A Narrative of Cultural Encounter in Southern China

A Narrative of Cultural Encounter in Southern China

Wu Xing Fights the Jiao

Hugh R. Clark

ANTHEM PRESS

Anthem Press

An imprint of Wimbledon Publishing Company
www.anthempress.com

This edition first published in UK and USA 2022
by ANTHEM PRESS
75–76 Blackfriars Road, London SE1 8HA, UK
or PO Box 9779, London SW19 7ZG, UK
and
244 Madison Ave #116, New York, NY 10016, USA

Copyright © Hugh R. Clark 2022

The author asserts the moral right to be identified as the author of this work.

All rights reserved. Without limiting the rights under copyright reserved above, no part of this publication may be reproduced, stored or introduced into a retrieval system, or transmitted, in any form or by any means (electronic, mechanical, photocopying, recording or otherwise), without the prior written permission of both the copyright owner and the above publisher of this book.

British Library Cataloguing-in-Publication Data
A catalogue record for this book is available from the British Library.

Library of Congress Control Number: 2022936470
A catalog record for this book has been requested.

ISBN-13: 978-1-83998-413-6- (Pbk)
ISBN-10: 1-83998-413-9 (Pbk)

This title is also available as an e-book.

This book is dedicated to my wife Barbara,
who has supported me throughout my career
and without whom there would be no career

CONTENTS

Relevant Dynastic Timeline — ix

Preface — x

1. Introduction to a Problem — 1
2. The Story — 17
3. Some Background — 31
4. The Sinitic Encounter and Wu Xing — 43
5. The Song Consolidation and Sinitic Accommodation — 55
6. The Ecological and Environmental Consequences — 65
7. Conclusions — 81

Suggestions for Further Reading — 89

Index — 91

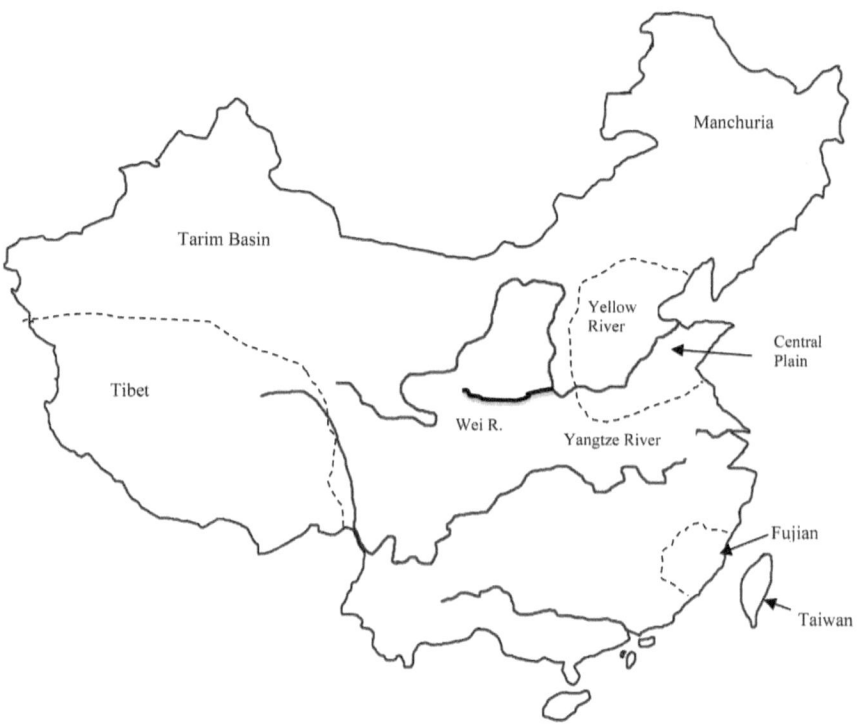

Map 0.1 Map of China, with key locations.

RELEVANT DYNASTIC TIMELINE

Neolithic Pre-History	? – ca.1500 BCE
Shang (or "Yin") dynasty	ca.1500 – 1046 BCE
Zhou dynasty	ca. 1046 BCE – 256 BCE
Western Zhou	ca. 1100 – 772 BC
Eastern Zhou	772 – 221 BCE
Spring & Autumn era	772 – 479 BCE
Warring States era	479 – 256 BCE
Rise of Qin	256 – 221 BCE
Qin dynasty	221 – 206 BCE
Han dynasty	206 BCE – 220 CE
Western Han	206 BCE – 9 CE
Wang Mang Interregnum	9 CE – 23 CE
Eastern Han	23 CE – 220 CE
Three Kingdoms (Wei, Shu Han, Wu)	220 CE – 280 CE
Jin dynasty	280 CE – 420 CE
Western Jin	280 CE – 316 CE
Eastern Jin	316 CE – 420 CE
Six dynasties	420 CE – 589 CE
Sui dynasty	581 CE – 618 CE
Tang dynasty	618 CE – 907 CE
Tang-Song Interregnum	878 CE – 978 CE
Song dynasty	960 CE – 1264 CE
Northern Song	960 CE – 1126 CE
Southern Song	1126 CE – 1279 CE
Yuan dynasty	1271 CE – 1368 CE
Ming dynasty	1368 CE – 1644 CE
Qing dynasty	1644 CE – 1912 CE

NOTE: Unless specified otherwise, all dates in this book are CE.

PREFACE

It has been about forty years since I first encountered the tale of Wu Xing and his battle with the *jiao* as I was researching my doctoral dissertation. As I shall discuss, Wu was directing a major project to drain a coastal salt marsh on the central Fujian coast. Having completed his project, so the narrative goes, the dikes that channeled fresh water through the newly reclaimed land were attacked by a *jiao*. Wu swore he would rescue his project by killing the beast—and beast it was. Wu grabbed his sword and plunged into the water to battle. After three days the *jiao* and Wu were both dead. The drainage project, however, was saved and to this day remains the core of one of China's most productive rice regions.

I have long found the story intrinsically interesting for its own sake at several levels. Who, for example, was Wu Xing, and why did he undertake such a massive project? What was its impact on the regional ecology and economy? What became of the people who had lived with the marsh before Wu drained it? These are all questions that link to wider themes, as I shall explain. Ultimately, however, there is a question that lies at the center of Wu Xing's tale: What is a *jiao*? It is at the core of the story, as I shall explain, yet no such creature exists in the natural world. Why does the story depend on such a mythological creature? Or could it in fact be something real?

Even if readers share my sense that these are interesting questions, none would be of much significance if there were not those broader themes, if there were not a broader insight to extract. Wu Xing's project, I will suggest, is a micro-event that provides insight into the much larger process whereby the vast reaches of southern China, the land that is drained by the middle and lower reaches of the Yangtze River basin as well as the adjacent littoral regions that frame that basin, were folded into the larger framework that today is China. Long ago the South, as I shall call that vast area, was home to a wide array of local and regional cultures. Although some endure to the present, especially in the uplands of the farther southwest, few retain the cultural authority they once had. For much of the last millennium the orthodox narrative, one that has been strongly embraced by the contemporary Chinese state, has maintained that the diverse cultures of the ancient south were subsumed into the single culture of the empire, within which they lost their distinct identity. As we shall see, however, it was not that simple. Although many ancient identities have been lost, cultural traits have survived and have helped shape what today we call "Chinese" culture. The micro-event that is Wu Xing and his battle with the *jiao* provides an opening through which we can consider the broader encounter between that imperial culture and the complex array of cultures that once controlled the South.

This encounter is one of the most important developments in the formation of China, yet until recently it has largely been overlooked. Through the course of the second and first millennia BCE an elite culture emerged out of the complex world of Neolithic cultures that once were spread across the Central, or "North China," Plain that flanks the lower reaches of the Yellow River in northern China. Through these centuries this culture, which I shall call "Sinitic" for it was not yet "Chinese," developed a body of literature and a related set of values, the so-called "classics" such as the *Documents*, the *Book of Poetry*, and the *Analects* of Master Kong (Confucius), that even today remains at the core of Chinese culture and identity. At the same time an array of southern cultures, some quite sophisticated and powerful but none with a well-developed system of writing, and so lacking the literary heritage that defined the Sinitic culture, had emerged with their contrasting set of values and identity. Although there had been contact between these two worlds for centuries if not even millennia, they met each other most directly through the first millennium CE, and the result transformed both.

The question of cultural encounter is not a uniquely Chinese issue. Every empire in human history has had to engage it at some level. The Romans met the Gauls, the Iberians and the Anglos as they spread their empire north and west, while to the east they navigated a complex relationship with the Greek culture. The Mongols ruled over both the Confucian lands of the Chinese empire and the Islamic world of Persia and Central Asia. The English engaged the disparate cultures of North America and sub-Saharan Africa as well as the mature culture of India. The Russians pressed into the Moslem lands of Central Asia and the widely disparate cultures of Siberia. In all such cases the standard narrative has favored the imperial culture. The elites of the Central Plain were not alone in asserting that their culture defined civilization Yet in all cases that culture has been affected by the cultures it has encountered. Cultural exchange is rarely a one-way phenomenon. How that exchange happened at least along the south central coast of China that today is Fujian is the topic of the book that follows.

Chapter 1
INTRODUCTION TO A PROBLEM

Many eons ago, long before the consolidation of the modern nation-state we call China, the southeastern quadrant of the Eurasian landmass that is China today was a complex world composed of myriad cultures of diverse origins. In the northern reaches of this region, across the vast alluvial plain formed by the eons of flooding by the Yellow River, known in Chinese texts as the Central Plain and to geographers as the North China Plain, a cluster of localized cultures had formed by the fourth to third millennia BCE. These cultures were complex and technologically sophisticated. By the early to middle second millennium a written language had evolved that enabled a narrow stratum of literate elites to share ideas and to nurture the development of a classical culture that is identified with figures such as Confucius. This culture was widely shared across the divergent cultures of the Plain, providing thereby a common bond. This is the nascent civilization that in this book we shall call Sinitic, so as not to confuse it with Chinese, which, as we shall argue, only emerged many centuries later. Concurrently, in the vast regions that lay south of the Plain and the Yellow River basin, an array of importantly and pronouncedly distinct but equally complex cultures had formed in the basin of the Yangtze River and its tributaries and along the coast south of the river's mouth. Traditionally, History has not recognized the contributions of these cultures to Chinese civilization. That is in part what this book intends to address.

Through the second millennium BCE the cultures of the Central Plain, one of the largest alluvial plains in the world, began to consolidate into a loosely homogenized whole in an era that historians know as the Shang, or Yin, dynasty. Regional differences across the Plain remained, but enough was shared that historians can realistically refer to this as the root from which Sinitic and then mature Chinese culture emerged. This consolidation, however, was limited to the Plain and the Yellow River drainage basin, including some tributary basins to the west. Even as patterns of interaction developed, especially along the lines of encounter, the cultures of the Yangtze basin and the adjacent coast largely remained both diverse and distinct.

Over time, as we all know, a new order took shape that united this vast realm with its great diversity into one holistic empire, an empire and now a modern nation-state that has replaced the old diversity with political unification and cultural homogenization. The book that follows explores a microcosm of history on the southeast coast to consider from multiple angles how that came to be. In the process I will challenge two perspectives that have both influenced the study of China's past: First, what we might call the presentist perspective, and second, the teleological perspective.

Presentism is the ahistorical assumption that what is today has always been, that we can apply what we know from our present to times past, that social relations, family structures and assumptions about how individuals of the past understood the world they lived in were no different from our own. It is an easy trap into which even historians, whose very training should reject it, fall prey. We all live, after all, in a present that offers a deceptive stability. Few who might read this book, for example, have ever lived in a time when the United States was not defined by its current borders,[1] when it was not among the wealthiest and most powerful of the world's nations, and it has been hard to imagine that it has not always been and will not always be so. That is presentism. Yet Americans are nearly universally familiar with the expansionist history of our nation from its beginnings as a fractious collection of politically insignificant colonies of widely varying levels of wealth on the Atlantic coast to its current spread from Florida to Alaska and Hawaii to Maine. Even as few on reflection would assert that the United States has always held its present position as one of the most dominant nations in the world, few are likely to foresee a major change in status in the future: What is always will be; the present defines both past and future.

The People's Republic of China, as the modern nation-state is known, is a similarly vast country, territorially almost exactly equivalent in size to the United States.[2] Because the history of that nation is so much less well known to us, it is easy to apply presentist presumptions and so to assume it has always been so. In fact, modern China is the result of a similar expansion and territorial assimilation, an historical fact that all too often even native Chinese historians have overlooked, yet it is essential to the definition of China as we know it today. If the United States expanded from a fractious collection of colonies on the eastern fringe of North America, the Chinese empire expanded

---

1 The last adjustment of American borders was in 1959 when Hawaii was admitted as the fiftieth state in the union.

2 Both the United States of America (including Alaska and Hawaii) and the People's Republic of China, as currently constructed, embrace about 3.7 million square miles.

from an equally fractious collection of principalities across the Central Plain. What is today has not always been, and often what has been is important to understanding what is. Good history avoids the presentist trap. Refuting a presentist perspective on China is a goal of this book.

The second trap that good history avoids, one that is closely related to presentism, is the teleological trap. Teleology means to be driven toward a definable end. It is derived from the Greek words *telos*, or end, and *logos*, meaning logic or knowledge. Teleological history is the premise that history moves toward a known destination. If presentism assumes "what is today always will be," the teleological perspective assumes that "what is today had to be."

All history in a very real sense is teleological: Historians cannot construct a narrative that leads to an outcome that differs from what has happened. We know the present, and it is the only outcome that we can know. We are aware of the inevitable outcome, even as we may argue about how it has come to be. No matter how creative one's imagination may be, the peoples of Mesoamerica did not open the trans-Atlantic sea lanes. Napoleon did not defeat Wellington at Waterloo, nor did Germany emerge from World War II victorious. Likewise, the nascent United States did expand from sea to shining sea, and the Chinese empire did expand to include the Yangtze basin and southeast coast. But none of these outcomes had to be until they had been. That is, until an outcome is accomplished, it does not have to be. Ironically but very meaningfully, only the past is teleological: For a historian the present is inevitable. Yet even as she knows how events unfolded: who won or lost; who went where and when; how technology has changed our world and so on, she must always bear in mind that until something was accomplished it did not have to be. The past did not have to unfold as it did, until it had. General Pickett did not have to lead his infamous charge, but once he did it could not not happen. It is the underlying premise of the present discussion, therefore, that the holistic empire, the China we know and have known all our lives, was not the only possible course of history.

To some the contested nature of several regions of the People's Republic, and so the possibility of alternative outcomes, is already familiar. Many, for example, are aware of modern China's contentious rule over Tibet, a vast highland plain, an altiplano, that sits behind a mountain barrier with an indigenous language and culture that is markedly distinct from those of contemporary China. For many centuries, Tibet had a theocratic government and a troubled and often hostile relationship with the Sinitic empire. Although it was invaded by the Mongols in the thirteenth century as part of their campaign to conquer all of the South and again by the Manchus in the eighteenth century in an effort to resist British colonial expansion from South Asia, these were transitory moments in the long history of the relationship. Its present stature as an integral part of the People's Republic was not settled—if, indeed, it can be called settled even now—until the People's Liberation Army invaded in 1959 with the intent of resolving Tibet's status permanently. Yet indigenous resistance to Beijing's rule and to the imposition of Chinese culture continues. Although our present reality, our presentist perspective, acknowledges that Tibet is under Chinese rule, it is possible, perhaps even likely, for history is long but human will is finite, that in time the relationship between the Chinese state and Tibet will change yet again, that new generations will grow up with a reality that has yet to be but will seem in their present to have always been.

Less well known is the relationship between the empire and the "New Frontier," or Xinjiang, the lands of the farther west that lie north of Tibet. If the latter is one of the world's highest plateaus, Xinjiang is defined by the Tarim Basin, a desert depression surrounded by some of the world's highest mountains: the Altai range to the west that separates it from Inner Asia, including Afghanistan; the Kunlun range that defines the edge of the Tibetan massif and the Mountains of Heaven, or Tian Shan, to the north. Although the Basin, cut off from atmospheric moisture by these ranges, is among the driest places on earth, along its perimeter runoff from the mountains that do catch moisture has provided water for a network of oasis communities.

Over two thousand years ago the Han dynasty laid claim to these communities, as did the Tang dynasty late in the first millennium CE; in between numerous peoples passed through this region from the west to lay claim to the Central Plain, the Sinitic heartland and its western peripheries. For many centuries thereafter the Basin had an uneasy but generally autonomous relationship with the empire until first the Mongols in the thirteenth century and then the Manchus in the later eighteenth century once again imposed imperial control. Although there have been times when Chinese authority has wavered, in a practical sense Xinjiang has been under Chinese authority since. However, just as the indigenous culture, language and even people of Tibet are distinctly not Chinese, nor are those of Xinjiang. The oasis communities have long been settled by peoples principally of Turkish heritage, especially Uighur and Tajik, whose culture, religion, food and language all draw on an Inner Asian heritage independent of Sinitic influence. And just as Tibet is regularly rocked by ethnic unrest, so is Xinjiang as the indigenous ethnic groups protest their subjugation to Chinese culture and authority.[3]

---

3 As this book is being written the Chinese state has incarcerated many thousands of indigenous Xinjiang natives, especially the Turkic Uyghur ethnic group, in re-education camps in an attempt to eradicate their indigenous culture and language and render them

There are other areas that carry distinct names bearing ethnic, cultural and linguistic significance: The southern extent of the vast Mongolian steppe that the contemporary Chinese state calls Inner Mongolia where grasslands dominate and the principle ethnic group remains Mongol, and Manchuria in the farther northeast, the ancient homeland of the Manchu people whose distinct ethnic identity, language and culture have been almost completely lost after several centuries of intimate commingling with the people and culture of greater China. Perhaps none is more relevant to the following discussion, however, than Taiwan, the island "nation" that lies off the southeast coast. From ancient times the inhabitants of the adjacent mainland coast have had contact with the island.[4] The earliest efforts to conquer and make the island a part of the mainland empire were in the early seventh century under the Sui dynasty (581–618), but full control was not asserted until the mid-seventeenth century. Under the Manchu Qing dynasty (1648–1912), the last imperial dynasty, the relationship between the mainland and the island underwent a profound change. For the first time Taiwan was considered a part of the empire. Initially it was under the administrative authority of Fujian province, but in the nineteenth century it was established as a distinct province. Through the Qing it became an outlet for population pressure on coastal Fujian, where inter-clan warfare contributed to making life precarious. In a pattern that echoes what we shall discuss in the chapters that follow on a much earlier time, migration out of Fujian across the Taiwan Strait, especially from the southern regions of the province on which this discussion focuses, transformed the demographic profile of the island. The indigenous non-Sinitic population was pushed into the interior mountains while the mainland immigrants took control of the agriculturally appealing lowlands. Late in the nineteenth century, as a consequence of the 1894–95 Sino-Japanese War, the island fell under Japanese control, which lasted until the end of World War II. Then in 1949, facing imminent defeat in the Chinese Civil War (1947–49), the Nationalists retreated to the island, where they have ever since maintained a distinct government that does not recognize the mainland government.[5]

---

loyal subjects of the government. Only time will tell to what extent this effort fulfills the government's goals.
4 See the collected essays in *Taiwan Maritime Landscapes from Neolithic to Early Modern Times*, edited by Paola Calanca, Frank Muyard, and Liu Yi-chang (Taipei: L'Ecole française d'Extrême-Orient, 2022).
5 Although the mainland government remains committed to reintegrating Taiwan into the national polity, as it forced the reintegration of Tibet and the Tarim Basin, at the time of this writing Taiwan remains self-governing.

These are the often contested regions of the modern Chinese state; their distinct histories are evident through their names. They are not, however, the subject of our present inquiry. That, rather, is a vast region that today is fully assimilated into both the culture and politics of China, a region with a long history predating its assimilation that is virtually unknown. That is the South, which was not always Chinese. How it became so is the central theme of what follows.

What is the South?

The history of China has long settled into a comfortable paradigm that has governed its study and that is central to the identity of the modern Chinese state. China is *Zhongguo*, the term that is commonly translated as "Middle Kingdom" and that today is the name of the Chinese state. The origins of the term are ancient, but it gained cultural meaning as the realm of civilization in the course of the first millennium BCE through the era known as the Zhou dynasty (ca. 1046–256 BCE). The dynasty had been established by peoples from the Wei River basin, a tributary to the Yellow River that for millennia has provided irrigation to a dry but fertile land bordering the western grasslands. Late in the second millennium BCE the Zhou peoples began to intrude upon—tradition says invaded, but the term may suggest something more directed and purposeful than what occurred—the Central Plain where the ruling family of the Shang dynasty had sat above a loosely coordinated network of local lords since the middle of the millennium. Ultimately the Zhou rulers deposed the Shang court and inherited its limited centralized authority. For several centuries the new order projected this authority from its homeland in the Wei River basin, until a further intrusion in the eighth century from the grasslands that lay beyond that basin forced the court to flee to the Plain. This relocation led to a collapse of the court's authority and the emergence of a congeries of autonomous, if not indeed independent, lords across the Plain, each with their own court and kingdom—each had, in Chinese terms, their own *guo*, a term that today translates the English term nation, but through the imperial era meant a court that was politically independent but ritually subordinate to a higher central authority. Although the Zhou court, absent an alternative, endured as that central pivot and focus of ritual subordination, in reality the center had no authority. In such a vacuum these lords competed with each other across centuries of intermittent but persistent warfare, an era that ultimately came to be known as the Warring States.

In this highly fluid but often violent context a legion of innovative thinkers who sought a way out of the morass developed a new cultural model; it was their model that in the discourse of the Central Plain came to define civilization. These included:

- Kong Fuzi (Confucius) and his heirs: Zengzi, Mengzi (or Mencius) and Xunzi,[6] who argued that the disorder stemmed from a loss of a moral standard that had flourished in the early Zhou era;
- Mozi and his band of specialists in defensive fortification whose influence from the fifth through third centuries BCE rivalled that of the Confucians, only to fade away when the chronic disorder itself was resolved when the Qin court forged a new unification, rendering their military expertise obsolete;
- the Legalists, whose authoritarian school was later rejected in name but which has provided the essential companion to the abstract moralizing of the Confucians for two millennia and
- the Daoists (or Taoists[7]), an eclectic movement of ill-defined origin that has long stood as a cultural counterpoint to Confucianism.

As this cultural model spread across the Plain, the term *Zhongguo* took on added meaning: The *Zhongguo*, the embracing term for the states across the Plain that is perhaps better rendered "the kingdoms (*guo*) in the center (*zhong*)" rather than the traditional "middle kingdom," was the full embodiment of civilization.[8] All other cultural models were, therefore, by definition inferior. To the apostles of this culture its appeal was so obvious, so overwhelming, that it was certain all who encountered it would inevitably adopt it. They did not need to proselytize their culture, for it would naturally spread.

It is in this context that the "comfortable paradigm" of Chinese history that is alluded to above took shape. Because the appeal of *Zhongguo* culture was deemed so obvious to the elites of the Plain, it was inconceivable that any who were exposed to it would ever choose to remain trapped by their "barbarian" heritage. And that brings us to the South. If the culture of the

---

6 The names Confucius and Mencius are Latinizations of the Chinese names Kong Fuzi, or "Celebrated Master" Kong, and Mengzi, or "Master" Meng, used by Jesuit interpreters at the time of their first contact with China in the sixteenth century. Although Xunzi was the equal to Mengzi in the ancient Confucian pantheon, by the time of the Jesuit contact Mengzi's optimistic interpretation of human nature had overcome Xunzi's somewhat darker perspective, so he was never awarded a Latinized name.
7 Transliteration of Chinese is among the banes of Chinese scholarship. For many years until the late 1970s scholars writing in English routinely used the Wade-Giles system; since then, under pressure from the Chinese government, Wade-Giles has been displaced by the *pinyin* system developed in the 1950s by Chinese linguists. This text uses *pinyin*, but when the Wade-Giles alternative is well known, as in Taoist (W-G) versus Daoist (*pinyin*), I will indicate that.
8 From their perspective these courts truly were at the center, surrounded by a sea of uncivilized barbarians. This is what the term in its origins meant.

Zhongguo defined civilization, then the South: the vast lands drained by the Yangtze River, fed by tributaries both from the river's north and south, as well as the entire coastline south of the Shandong Peninsula and stretching all the way to the Red River delta of modern Vietnam,[9] was populated by the uncivilized, the "barbarian." It was widely, if not universally believed among the "civilized" elite of the *Zhongguo*, however, that civilization was at least partially defined by values, not ethnicity, and values can be learned. Those uncivilized southern barbarians could become civilized, just as the Zhou "conquerors" had as they encountered the ancient culture of Shang from which civilization derived.

It is from this premise that through the middle centuries of the first millennium BCE *Zhongguo* scholars acknowledged a new kingdom, or *guo*, as a participant in the affairs of the civilized world. This was Chu, centered on the plains lying north of the central Yangtze valley in modern Hubei. The acknowledgment by those northern scholars that Chu scholars were a participant in their philosophical debates and that the Chu court was involved in the politics of the Central Plain was the first time that civilization was deemed to have at least partially supplanted southern barbarism.

In the diverse world of the South, Chu was distinct. Influenced by the political structures of the *Zhongguo*, Chu took on the essential trappings of a *guo*: a central court organized around a single ruler who exercised power through a proto-bureaucracy. The Chu elite gained fluency in both the ideographic orthography of the Central Plain—what we call "Chinese characters"—and the associated cultural discourse, a discourse that was transmitted in written form. Begrudgingly, the scholarly culture of the *Zhongguo* accepted Chu as a contributor. Yet Chu culture remained distinct, as is expressed in eponymous texts such as the *Songs of Chu* (Chu ci) but also in the *Book of Master Zhuang* (Zhuangzi), which along with the *Classic of the Way and Virtue* (Daode jing) is considered one of the foundational texts of Daoism. If Confucius illustrated the phlegmatic nature of northern culture when he famously told his followers that he had nothing to say about the spirit world, Chu culture embraced the ecstatic and numinous. In the *Songs* and the *Book of Master Zhuang* we meet ghosts, we accompany Sages on out-of-body excursions that course throughout the cosmos, and we are urged to survive on diets of morning dew and

---

9 For a thousand years from the late first millennium BCE until the end of the first millennium CE Chinese courts claimed authority over the Red River basin and spread an overlay of Sinitic culture, including the name, on an otherwise non-Sinitic population. This legacy persists even today in the extensive Sino-Vietnamese vocabulary as well as in the Confucian temple that is a tourist mainstay in Hanoi.

vaporous ethers. As Ban Gu (32–92 CE) wrote of southern culture and people in his *Book of Han*, in a trope that came to epitomize northern perception of the southern barbarians, "They put faith in shamans and demons and embrace barbaric rites."[10]

Elsewhere within the nearer regions of the South similar trappings also began to evolve, but with a very different response from the northern scholars. Most notably, in the area of modern Jiangsu province that lies between the Shandong Peninsula and the Yangtze delta, adjacent to and heavily influenced by the culture of the *Zhongguo*, a kingdom known as Wu emerged.[11] Sima Qian (ca. 145–ca. 86 BCE), called the "father of Chinese historiography," devoted a chapter to the royal house of Wu in his seminal *Records of the Grand Historian*. However, although Sima claimed the family was descended from the Zhou royal family and so drew on an ancient heritage of civilization, he distinguished between the rulers of the *Zhongguo*, who were kings (*wang*), and the rulers of Wu, whom he defined as princes (*tai bo*). Their subjects, he emphasized, were barbarians who lacked the civilized principles of the *Zhongguo*; rulers of such people could not be kings. Thus, although Wu, like Chu, had a royal court that used Sinitic orthography to correspond with the kingdoms of the Plain, the land was never considered civilized and could not be counted among the *Zhongguo*.[12]

Scholars also recognized a *guo* they called Yue on the south shore of the Hangzhou Bay, but whether it truly merited such status is debatable. The *Zhongguo* scholars were mostly enthralled by a man they knew as Goujian.[13]

---

10 *Han shu* 28b:141b.
11 It is worth remembering that all our standard pronunciations are in the contemporary Chinese we call Mandarin. In fact, among the scholars of the later first millennium BCE who compiled the early records the kingdom's name would have been pronounced something closer to Ngu, very likely with hard finial, thus something like ŋu-k.
12 *Shi ji* chapter 31. Sima referred to the people of Wu as *yi man*, both of which are ancient terms used to refer to non-Sinitic peoples of the frontier. As a compound they mean "eastern barbarians."
13 We only know of Goujian through Sinitic literature, the only literature that was extent. As a native of the Hangzhou Bay region, it is likely that his native language was not the language of the Sinitic world, which itself was as yet very diverse; in all probability it was derivative of the Proto-Austronesian languages that were indigenous to the southeast coast. Sinitic literature, bound by the limits of Sinitic orthography, had no convenient way to render alien sounds or names except by using characters approximating the sound. Thus, we can only presume that Goujian was an approximate rendering of the man's name. Following on a previous footnote, a further complication is that Goujian is the modern pronunciation of the characters that the ancient Sinitic scribes used; 2,500 years ago their pronunciation would have been quite different. Thus, we do not really know the name of this man, only how it was transcribed in ancient literature.

He was a charismatic tribal leader who rallied the peoples through the region that today is northern Zhejiang province into a confederation. He launched successful campaigns against both Chu and Wu and sought to intervene in the politics of the Plain.[14] Sima Qian even granted Goujian the title king (*wang*) that he denied to the rulers of Wu. But Goujian's confederation appears to have been anchored on his charisma and to have slowly dissolved after his death; although history notes subsequent kings of the Yue, they play a far less influential role. Much further south in the Pearl River estuary in the vicinity of modern Guangzhou (Canton) there may have been yet another organized polity, although little is known.

What we can conclude is that throughout the classical era of Shang and Zhou relations between the "civilized" Central Plain and the nearer south were complex, but as one moved deeper into the "barbaric" far south they were few and the influence of one on the other was increasingly limited. Beyond these scattered polities the rest of the South lacked organized state structures. The interior river valleys that fed the Yangtze were occupied by diverse tribal cultures collectively known to the scholars of the Plain as *man*—a generalized and dismissive ethnonym commonly applied to the indigenous inhabitants of the southern interior but with little specific meaning. If state structures were lacking, technological and social sophistication were not. Indeed, some of the earliest pottery in human history, yielding carbon dates as early as 20,000 before present (BP), came from these river valleys. Likewise, inhabitants of several sites associated with the Neolithic cultures of these valleys had definitively developed agriculture by early in the last deca-millennium BP.[15] They may have been stateless, but they were not without their accomplishments.

A similar array of cultures lived along the long coastline between the Hangzhou Bay and Pearl River estuary; northern scholars commonly and collectively called these cultures *yue*—the name of Goujian's kingdom.[16] Although *yue*, like *man*, is a dismissive ethnonym with little explicit meaning, there are certain generalizations that are commonly accepted. For example, although the *yue* peoples were in fact very diverse and lacked any

---

14 As a result, Goujian has left a fascinating imprint on Chinese culture that endures to the present. On this see Paul A. Cohen, *Speaking of History: The Story of King Goujian in Twentieth-Century China* (Berkeley: University of California Press, 2008).
15 David Joel Cohen, "The Beginnings of Agriculture in China: A Multiregional View," *Current Anthropology* 52, no. S4, The Origins of Agriculture: New Data, New Ideas (October 2011): S276–S278.
16 To a significant degree *man* and *yue* are interchangeable. The convenient contrast I outline between the two terms is best taken as a useful heuristic device rather than a hard and fast rule.

integrating polity beyond confederations such as that engineered by Goujian, many are believed to have spoken languages belonging to the earliest stages of the Austronesian language family—what linguists commonly call Proto-Austronesian,[17] suggesting some possible deeper affinity that had disappeared by the dawn of their recorded history. They broadly appear to have shared a belief in the power of nature and the numinous, although such beliefs are hardly unusual in human experience and need not point to any shared heritage. Economically the *yue* peoples had diverse practices. Riziculture, the cultivation of rice, was common and in some areas wetland cultivation had developed as early as 7,000–8,000 BP—an anticipation of the sophisticated agriculture of more recent times that relies on the technologically challenging paddy (or *padi*) field, of which more below. All *yue* peoples supplemented whatever agriculture they practiced with hunting and gathering. Most particularly relevant to the story we are going to focus on, those along the coast depended on the products of the sea for their livelihoods. For many that meant exploiting the coastal marshes and shallow seas, but some in addition developed the ability to exploit deep-water resources. In fact, the predominant anthropological opinion today argues that it was the peoples of modern southeast China and Taiwan who, taking advantage of their deep-water, open-ocean skills, settled the islands of the Pacific where Austronesian languages dominate.[18]

Through the mid- to late third century BCE the kingdoms of the *Zhongguo* were brought under the unified rule of the Qin dynasty (the dynastic dates: 221–206 BCE, begin with the proclamation of the dynasty, but the process of unification by conquest began several decades earlier). Contrary to the assumptions of *Zhongguo* civilization, however, this was not done through cultural conversion but by military conquest. For several centuries, the Qin kingdom, which had emerged in the Wei River valley from where Zhou had launched its takeover of the Plain almost a millennium earlier, had maintained an uneasy relationship with the civil culture of the Plain. Although Qin was considered one among the *Zhongguo*, like Chu its claim to belong to the world of the civilized was never fully accepted by the morally judgmental academic culture of the Plain. As Zhou had a millennium earlier, Qin drew

---

17 Today the Austronesian family of languages stretches from the Central Pacific to Madagascar. Most scholars trace the roots of this family to southeastern China, from where it spread to Taiwan and then into Southeast Asia and the Pacific. It is important to distinguish between language and culture. The Austronesian language family embraces a huge array of diverse cultures.

18 The most thorough English-language discussion of the ancient *yue* is Erica Fox Brindley, *Ancient China and the Yue* (Cambridge, UK: Cambridge University Press, 2015).

on the martial qualities of the grasslands; the Qin elite, although conversant in the civil discourse of the *Zhongguo*, never abandoned their martial aggressiveness. Beginning in the middle decades of the third century BCE, the kingdom commenced a step-by-step campaign to bring the entire *Zhongguo* under its rule, concluding in 221 when the king of Qin proclaimed for himself the grandiose title "First Emperor" (*Shi Huangdi*).[19]

Although Qin rule was short lived, following the complete subjugation of the *Zhongguo* it was the first power from the Plain to launch a campaign of subjugation against the South. The campaign was only a qualified success: Although Qin authority was established at key nodes, especially in the river valleys linking the Yangtze basin to the deepest south, the so-called South of the Mountains (Lingnan) from where the exotic goods of the South China Sea could be accessed, Qin armies suffered horrific losses, especially as they faced the unfamiliar pathogens of the southern environment. In the face of this new power, moreover, the myriad cultures of the South maintained their distinct identity in contrast to northern culture. Even when Qin was succeeded by Han (206 BCE–220 CE) and the new rulers inherited the empire, the south remained a land apart, a land where a very thin overlay of Sinitic culture coexisted with a deep base of non-Sinitic regional cultures, languages and beliefs. The South was gradually incorporated politically, but it remained culturally distinct.

The veneer of unified empire began to dissolve late in the second century CE when a pair of Daoist-inspired rebellions simultaneously broke out. Shandong, in the heart of the old *Zhongguo*, was wracked by the Yellow Turbans, an uprising that drew on a long heritage of proto-Daoist millenarian movements that had flourished in the region for at least two centuries. Sichuan, far to the west, was beset by the Celestial Masters, a faith-healing movement that drew heavily on the dominant non-Sinitic population of the region's highlands.[20] Although neither movement managed to overthrow the dynasty, the court never recovered its authority. Technically the Han endured until 220, but for three to four decades it existed as little more than a shell. When the last Han emperor was overthrown, the empire broke into three

---

19 "Emperor" is the standard translation of the term *huangdi*, but it may not be the best term. Increasingly scholars have rendered it "thearch," or "divine ruler," to emphasize the *huangdi*'s role as the link between the cosmos (*tian*) and humankind. Because "emperor" is the long-time standard while "thearch" is to most an unfamiliar term, we shall stick with the former while keeping in mind the implications of the latter.
20 On this and the following, see Barbara Hendrichke, "Early Daoist Movements," in *Daoism Handbook*, Volume 1, edited by Livia Kohn (Leiden: E.J. Brill, 2004), 134–143. See also Terry Kleeman, *Celestial Masters: History and Ritual in Early Daoist Communities* (Cambridge, MA: Harvard University Asia Center, 2016).

parts: Wei, governing the old land of the *Zhongguo*; (Shu) Han in Sichuan; and Wu in the Yangtze basin. Collectively they are known in the orthodox record as the Three Kingdoms. Other than a brief and inconclusive unification in the late third century, the holistic empire was not fully reimposed until a northern general named Yang Jian brought North and South together in the late sixth century under the Sui dynasty.

Although this is not the place to detail the arcane and complex politics of those centuries,[21] there are a couple of general points that are important. First, and perhaps most importantly, although the orthodox narrative describes the end of this era of division as a "restoration" of holistic empire, note that I have said it was "reimposed." In the long span of history, the four centuries of the holistic Qin/Han empire are in fact the interruption. Never before had there been such an empire; the return to an era of division, an era that lasted almost as long as the holistic Qin/Han empire, was in fact a reversion to an historical norm. Because the elites of Wu and the successive dynasties that followed in the Yangtze basin drew heavily on relocated branches of elite northerners who brought their culture with them, an overlay of Sinitic values took root, especially in the region of the southern capital at Jiankang (modern Nanjing). To what extent these elites dreamed of reunifying with the North is debatable; some undeniably did, but others seem to have been content with their southern realm. What is clear is that throughout the centuries between the collapse of the Han and the holistic empire of Sui/Tang (589–907), despite moments of conflict between the northern and southern empires, there was no concerted effort to reestablish the holistic empire from either.

No doubt one reason for this is that below the veneer of elite Sinitic culture indigenous cultures persisted. Through the centuries of the southern dynasties, moreover, the once distinct Sinitic elite merged more and more with indigenous elites, which included both families fully native to the South with no heritage of Sinitic identity and others who through the preceding centuries had migrated into the Yangtze basin from the old *Zhongguo* and adopted local cultural patterns. In short, between the collapse of Han in the early third century and rise in the late sixth century of the following era of holistic empire under the Sui/Tang empire, a culture and political tradition that drew heavily on indigenous cultural tropes flourished in the South that self-consciously saw itself as distinct from the politics and culture of the North.

---

21 Two recent books do an excellent job of this: Mark Edward Lewis, *China Between Empires: The Northern and Southern Dynasties* (Cambridge: The Belknap Press of Harvard University Press, 2009), and Andrew Chittick, *The Jiankang Empire in Chinese and World History* (Oxford: Oxford University Press, 2021).

But that only tells part of the story, for the South remained extremely diverse. If a hybrid elite culture drawing on both orthodox Sinitic and heterodox southern traditions took shape in the core of the Yangtze basin where the southern dynastic presence was strongest, as one moved beyond that core the values of the capital elite had less and less influence and culture became more and more alien, more and more indigenous. The southern elites who congregated around Jiankang, for example, shared the literate culture of the North that provided dynastic legitimization. Beyond the elite, on the other hand, there was no literary tradition; local cultures defined themselves through an oral heritage.

When the rulers of the Sui dynasty that gained control of the Central Plain in the later sixth century made the reimposition of holistic empire a policy goal, therefore, it was an initiative that came out of the North, out of the old *Zhongguo* and the heart of the Qin/Han empire, not out of any driving desire among southern elites for reunification with the ancient Sinitic heartland. It was also an initiative driven less by memories of holistic empire than a desire of the new court to access the growing wealth of the Yangtze basin, a region of surplus grain production and expanding foreign trade. The most enduring legacy of the Sui dynasty, in fact, was and is construction of the Grand Canal in order to facilitate shipment of the surplus grains and exotic products of the South to the northern capital. The lower reaches of the Yangtze basin were becoming rich, and the new imperial order intended to gain access to that wealth. Arguably, the new order had to have that access if it was to survive.

Like militarized Qin, which was followed so soon by Han, so militarized Sui, which had forcibly conquered the South, was soon after displaced by the Tang dynasty. And just as history regards Han as the civil resolution to Qin's violence, so Tang is presented as the civil resolution to the violence of the Sui conquest. Although the new court inherited the holistic empire that Sui had reimposed, however, the cultural division between North and South remained salient.

There was, of course, change. Through the nearly three centuries of the Tang, for example, the integration of northern and southern economies that prompted Sui construction of the Grand Canal advanced, as did the integration of southern elites into the orthodox culture that continued to be defined by the North. Yet at a personal level men of the North remained puzzled and alienated by the South.[22] Illustratively, the court dispatched its political exiles to the South, especially and most punitively to the deep South, the "land south of the mountains," as the deepest South was known. For northerners

---

22 See, for example, the eloquent examination of northern attitudes toward the South by Edward H. Schafer, *The Vermilion Bird: T'ang Images of the South* (Berkeley: University of California Press, 1967).

who suffered the indignity of exile, the "lands south of the mountains" were a threatening world of incomprehensible customs and unfamiliar dangers. Confronted with a range of pathogens to which they had no resistance, what William McNeill, with an explicit reference to China, once called a "steep disease gradient,"[23] they were expected to die, as so many did.

Yet to a growing number of anonymous men and women, the South was a beckoning land of opportunity. Throughout the Tang, and especially in the decades following the mid-eighth-century uprising known as the An Lushan Rebellion when the North was thrown into violent turmoil, when the court had to flee its capital and find temporary refuge in the far west, when many of the population registers, used by the Tang to limit mobility and collect taxes, were destroyed, the registered population of the South grew.

Two factors must have contributed to this growth. Taxes were levied on the individual, and so could only be collected on households whose members were registered. We can imagine, therefore, that local officials across the South were eager to register indigenous households, but registration required permanence. We are restricted to impressionistic evidence about the nature of many indigenous cultures across the South, but in regions such as eastern Guangdong and southern Fujian, the regions where our story will focus and where material development appears to have lagged behind other regions, that evidence points to non-nucleated mobility. These were slash-and-burn agriculturalists and migratory fishermen. Some no doubt adapted to the expectations of "civilized" culture and became villagers, but many must have remained beyond the reach of the registers, a population as we shall see that both figuratively and literally remained afloat.

The second source of the expansion in registered population was immigrants. These were people who could have come from almost anywhere, but collectively they illustrated a broad population shift from north to south, driven by both turmoil and opportunity. No doubt they reflected a wide range of cultural traditions, but a significant number brought with them the assumptions of Sinitic culture. They were agriculturalists—peasants who sought land and opportunity, and in growing numbers they found both in the coastal plains and riverine valleys that offered the best land. Gradually at first, but in a growing wave, they were transforming the South. It is that transformation to which we shall turn in the chapters that follow.

---

23 *Plagues and Peoples* (Garden City, NY: Anchor Press, 1976).

Chapter 2

THE STORY

The previous chapter lays out a wide-ranging background through a narrative that broadly illustrates the distinct history of the South, but the event through which our narrative is framed is defined narrowly and by a specific place. To understand the implications of that narrative, we need the story. Late in what we now call the eighth century CE, during the first year of the Restoration of Balance reign period of the Tang dynasty (the Restoration of Balance reign period was 780–84; the Tang dynasty was 618–906[1]), Wu Xing, whose identity we will consider below, organized a project centered on the Distributed Blessings Retention Dam to drain a coastal marsh. Located on the Plain of Emerging Transformation in Putian District on China's central coast in the area that in the years ahead came to be known as Fujian province (see Map 2.1), this was a complex project involving the damming of the Distributed Blessings Creek, the drainage of coastal salt marshes and distribution of fresh water through a network of canals into the now dry marshland (see Map 2.2). Wu's project was essential to the transformation of the Plain from a lightly settled wetland primarily utilized by non-Sinitic indigenous peoples into one of the most densely settled and economically productive areas of the empire. It is that transformation, a microcosm of transformation that was occurring across southern China through the first millennium CE, on which we are going to focus.

In his *New History of the Tang Dynasty*, compiled in the mid-eleventh century and regarded as one of the most authoritative accounts of the Tang, Ouyang Xiu (1007–1072) provided the earliest surviving reference to the

---

1 "Reign names" (*nian hao*) were proclaimed by emperors on taking the throne and thereafter throughout their reign whenever emperors felt it important to mark a particular moment or, as in this case, to announce a new initiative. Chinese historical records are organized by reign names. Thus the year marked 780 CE in the Gregorian calendar is referred to as "the first year of Restoration of Balance" in Chinese records, usually without explicit reference to the dynasty.

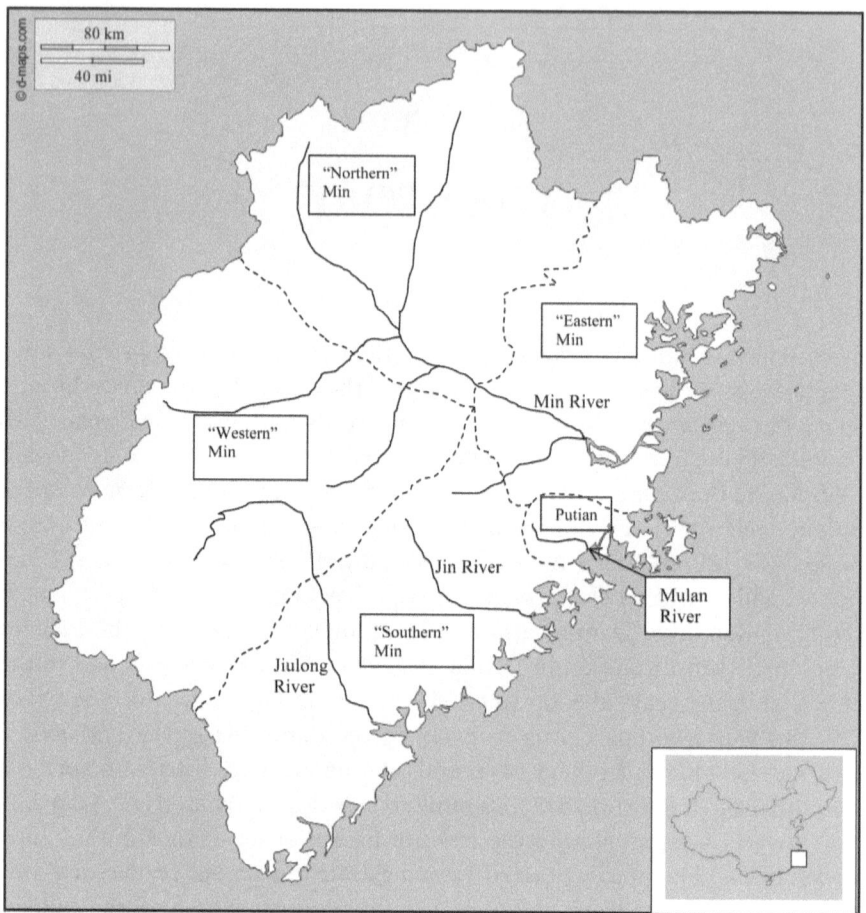

Map 2.1 Fujian outline, showing regions and major rivers (approximate). Source: d-maps.com, with inserted text.

project, although without reference to Wu Xing.[2] Ouyang recorded that the dam provided irrigation to "over 400 *qing*" (1 *qing* = 100 *mu* = ca. 150 acres; i.e., a total of ca. 6,000 acres), a sizable area itself, but later sources record that "over 2000 *qing*," or roughly 30,000 acres, were irrigated, the result of later additions to the network of canals.

There is very little we can say definitively about Wu Xing. There is no evidence that he held any official position, although at some point, perhaps

---

2 Ouyang Xiu, ed., *Xin Tangshu* [New History of the Tang Dynasty] (Beijing: Zhonghua shuju, 1975), 41:1065.

THE STORY 19

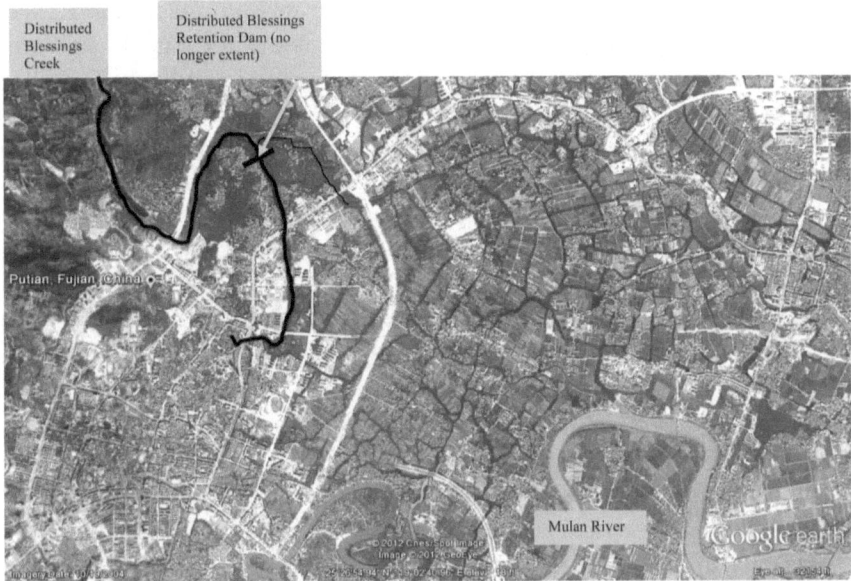

Map 2.2 Distributed Blessings Retention Dam and related irrigation network (Plain of Emerging Transformation, modern). Source: Google Earth, with inserted text and highlighting.

posthumously and probably by local custom only, he was granted the honorary title Commander (*chang guan*).[3] Nevertheless, he was able to marshal the considerable labor such a project required. Under his direction the creek was damned, itself no mean feat, and its water diverted. Through a complex web of canals and retention ponds, roughly 6,000 acres that had been a coastal salt marsh was drained and supplied with fresh water. Commander Wu was clearly both influential and a man of wealth. In Putian in the eighth century, which had yet to see the vast commercial revolution that transformed the local and regional economies in later centuries, this almost certainly means he was a major landowner, a conclusion that is consistent with his plans to convert salt marsh into land that could be used for agriculture. This was entirely consistent as well with the preference of the influx of Sinitic immigrants who had arrived in growing numbers in the aftermath of the traumatic An Lushan

---

3 Contemporary websites, drawing on modern genealogies of the Wu lineage, claim that Wu Xing's father was a native of Distributed Blessing District in Chang Prefecture of modern Jiangsu. He was a merchant who traveled to Putian; Wu Xing followed. See, for example, http://fj.sina.com.cn/city/putian/information/z/2012-11-20/10051133.html. While possible, the evidence is poor and unreliable.

Rebellion. The Sinitic economy at its root was an agricultural economy; these new settlers wanted land. Wu Xing was a champion of these goals, a conclusion that strongly suggests if he was not ethnically Sinitic himself, he had embraced the premises of Sinitic culture.

So much is based on circumstantial evidence. One reason we are left with such a level of uncertainty is that the earliest substantive discussion of Wu Xing and his project, an inscription composed in the mid-1250s to commemorate restoration of the local shrine dedicated to Wu Xing and his project, was written nearly 500 years later. Liu Kezhuang (1187–1269), the author, was a prolific essayist whose collected works are one of the most important sources on local history. His commemorative inscription is the place for us to begin:

> According to the prefectural gazetteer, the network was first built in the Restoration of Balance era of the Tang dynasty. ...[4] Of old, before the dam was built, the tidal flow came as far as Shihua Bridge.[5] [Wu Xing] dammed off the seas and blocked the tides; he channeled the streams to irrigate the land, turning saline lands into who knows how many thousand, even tens of thousands, of *qing* of fertile fields.[6]

---

4 Gazetteers are an essential source for local history. Although few texts survive, the genre already had a long history by the end of the first millennium CE (see D. Jonathan Felt, *Structures of the Earth: Metageographies of Early Medieval China* [Cambridge, MA: Harvard University Asia Center, 2021]). Under the Song dynasty (960–1279) gazetteers developed to include a wide range of information such as administrative history, surveys of important geographic sites including mountains and rivers, and biographies of important figures who either served in the local administration or were natives of the locality, all of which were thought to be useful to the administrative officials assigned to the local jurisdictions these works covered. The earliest Putian gazetteer was compiled in 1192 by, among others, Liu Kezhuang's father Liu Mizheng, and that is no doubt the text Liu Kezhuang referred to. In the omitted text Liu repeats—and accepts—a tradition that the dam had been built as early the beginning of the eighth century; I believe this is inconsistent with the history of the area, and it is rejected in later sources, so I omit it here.

5 Huang Zhongzhao, *BaMin tongzhi* [Comprehensive gazetteer of the Eight Districts of Fujian] (Fuzhou: Fujian renmin chubanshe, 1990; henceforth BMTZ), 19:380, compiled in 1491, notes of the Shihua Bridge: "It was north of the prefectural city ... It no longer exists." This is consistent with the location of the dam, which is also north of the prefectural city.

6 See Liu Kezhuang, *Houcun xiansheng daquanji* [Fully Complete Collection of the Works of the Master Behind the Village] (Sibu conggan ed. [henceforth SBCG], 92:16b–18b; see also *Putian shuili zhi* [Record of water conservancy in Putian], compiled by Chen Maolie [Taibei: Chengwen chubanshe 1974 reprint of 1875 edition; hereafter PTSLZ], 8:23a–24a and *Epigraphical Materials on the History of Religion in Fujian: Xinghua Region*, edited

A bit more detail on the project itself survives in a much later inscription compiled in 1538 to commemorate a further restoration to the shrine:

> [The Distributed Blessings Retention Dam] is the work of Wu Xing. In the Restoring the Balance era of the Tang the people's natures were generous and embraced virtue. Before this the several streams of Xinghua prefecture flowed to the east into the Distributed Blessings Creek, [from where] they flowed out of the retaining ponds and into the sea. Official Wu blocked off the sea and created fields. Then he built a long dike to direct the flow [of the streams] into the coastal retaining ponds to store water, which poured forth for irrigation of more than 2000 *qing* of fields.[7]

Before construction of the Distributed Blessings Retention Dam and its modern descendants, much of the flood plain of the lower Mulan River and its adjacent tributaries such as the Distributed Blessings Creek was a coastal marsh that offered little dry land suitable for agriculture. Thus the potential return on draining its soils remained unrealized. By the thirteenth century the Shihua Bridge that was referenced by Liu Kezhuang was already a long-lost structure that once lay north of the district city; it had been rendered unnecessary by coastal reclamation projects such as Wu Xing's that turned the estuaries of the coastal marsh, which it presumably had crossed, into dry land. The 1538 inscription implies that before Wu's project there had been some attempts to corral the waters coming off the hills surrounding the northern plain: "the [runoff of the] several streams … flowed out to the retaining ponds and then into the sea."

The Distributed Blessings Retention Dam was the first and most important of a series of projects that controlled the flooding and opened the land to the dense settlement and intensive exploitation that had already developed by the eleventh and twelfth centuries. Through a network of dikes and retention ponds that checked the tidal incursions that had rendered much of the marsh a saline wasteland, the dam and its linked network of canals brought fresh water to the now drained land. In recognition of Wu's success, in the centuries between his death in the later eighth century and Liu's mid-thirteenth-century

---

by Kenneth Dean and Zheng Zhenman (Fuzhou: Fujian renmin chubanshe, 1996; henceforth Dean & Zheng, *Xinghua*), 55–56.

Liu's claim of "many thousand, even tens of thousands, of *qing* of fertile fields" is a reflection of the reclamation of much additional land in the decades and centuries following Wu Xing's initial project; we will return to this in Chapter 5.

7 Zheng Yue, "Wu changguan miao xiusi bei" [Stele commemorating restoration of the shrine of Official Wu], PTSLZ 8:25a–26a; also in Dean & Zheng, *Xinghua*, 167–68.

inscription he was honored with an ever more impressive series of posthumous titles conferred by imperial decree:

> In the Grand Perspective era (1107-1110) of the [Song] dynasty, an [imperial] placard was conferred on the shrine, and in the era of On-going Revival (1131-1162) [Wu Xing] was enfeoffed "Just and Brave Marquis." In the era of Divine Intervention (1241-1252) "Universal Assistance" was added to his title, and his wife was enfeoffed "Lady of Manifest Benevolence." [Finally] in the Era of Precious Intervention (1253-1258) there was a request for his ennoblement, and an imperial edict proclaimed his accomplishments to all the world.[8]

Liu's inscription was a commemoration of the final award, the public proclamation of Wu's posthumous ennoblement in the 1250s, in preparation for which the restoration commemorated by Liu had been undertaken.

But once Wu's project had been completed, something went horribly wrong. What had initially been presented as a straightforward and thoroughly secular historical narrative suddenly takes a turn. Let's start again with Liu Kezhuang:

> When the project was complete, a wrathful *jiao* broke the dikes. But the poor and rootless one (i.e., Wu Xing) expelled the evil. His accomplishment stands in history like those of Li Bing and Zhou Chu.[9]

Liu then added a poem:

> Soon after [he had completed the dikes], beneath the maelstrom
> There was a winding, wiggling creature.
> The Marquis grabbed his precious knife
> And clenched his empty fist.
> Donating his worthless body,
> He looked over the unfathomable abyss.
> The evil that lay within the water was dead,
> And the Golden Dike was firm.
> I have heard the immortals of ancient times

---

8 Liu Kezhuang, *Houcun xiansheng daquanji* 92:16b–18b.
9 Li Bing lived during the Warring States era and saved the state of Shu from a catastrophic flood. Zhou Chu, who lived in the third century CE following the Han dynasty, battled both a ferocious tiger and a *jiao*, conquering both and rectifying his own wayward ways.

Must all have done meritorious acts
If they were to ride the wind and rain
And ascend to the Great Source.
Yet the marvel of Wu Guang's sacrifice,[10]
The injustice of throwing [oneself] in the Xiang River,[11]
Or riding on the back of the Great Peng Bird,[12]
How can they compare to submitting to the saliva of a hungry *jiao*?

The late fifteenth-century *Comprehensive Gazetteer of the Eight Districts of Fujian* offered a more prosaic if equally imaginative version:

> Wu Xing grabbed a sword and told the people, "If the water runs blue-green than the *jiao* is dead, but if it runs red, then I am dead." Then he entered the water and battled the demon. Three days later a blade covered in blood washed up on Wu's Sword Beach. Wu and the demon were both dead.[13]

Finally, Zheng Yue, author of the 1538 inscription quoted above (see Note 7), was brief:

> At this time there was a *jiao* that was terrorizing the people. Official Wu swore an oath to the people that with his sword he would enter the water and kill the *jiao*. But both he and the *jiao* died.

Where the story of Wu Xing and the Distributed Blessings Retention Dam is both secular and real, with the *jiao* the tale of Wu Xing veers into the unreal, the mythological. Tradition insists that having drained about 6,000 acres of marshland, Wu was confronted by a "winding, wiggling" and "hungry" *jiao*, a horrific beast that was terrifying the people as it was destroying the embankments on which the project depended. To save Wu's project, the *jiao* had to be killed. But what is a *jiao*?

A beast by this name has a long history in classical Chinese literature, with references throughout the classical tradition, including philosophical works

---

10 A reference to the legend of Wu Guang, to whom Tang, the last of the legendary rulers of the ancient past, was going to give his kingdom. Rather than accept, Wu Guang drowned himself.
11 A reference to the legend of Qu Yuan, the ancient poet who threw himself into the Xiang River in the face of unjust accusations.
12 A reference to the tale in the *Book of Master Zhuang* of the Great Peng Bird.
13 BMTZ, 60:410.

such as the *Book of Changes* (Yi jing), ritual guides such as the *Book of Rites* (Li ji), natural compendia such as the *Classic of Mountains and Streams* (Shanhai jing) and even essentially secular historical texts such as the *Records of the Grand Historian* (Shi ji). The *Discussion of Writing and Explanation of Characters* (Shuowen jiezi), compiled in the second century CE and often described as the first Chinese dictionary, identifies the *jiao* as "a kind of dragon (*long*)," noting that it can both "swim like a fish and fly."[14] A commentary on the "Poetical description of the Shu capital" (Shudu fu) of Zuo Si (250–305), one of the most influential prose poems of the Jin Dynasty, refers to the *jiao* as a "water spirit,"[15] while elsewhere the beast is specifically linked to floods.[16]

Tang scholars and poets added to the legend of the *jiao*—sometimes called instead a *jiaochi* or simply *chi*—which they generally identified with the Farther South. The famous essayist and scholar Liu Zongyuan (773–819), for example, tells of such a beast he called a *jiaochi* that terrorized the people of Yongzhou (Guangnan west): "It had destroyed the river bank right up to the city gate. It overturned boats and killed the people, and then went away. The elders lamented, '… It can enter fire and not move. It's a god (*shen*[17]). We have been under its thrall for ten years.'"

Invocation of *jiao* is in fact quite common in classical literature. Like Liu, his colleague Han Yu (768–824), the most famous essayist of the later Tang, alluded to the *jiao* frequently. At the height of his career early in the ninth century Han fell afoul of court politics and suffered the indignity of exile to Chaozhou, the remote and alien coastal prefecture in eastern Guangdong province that abuts Zhangzhou prefecture in Fujian and so is not far from Wu Xing's project.[18] While there he wrote of the creature in numerous poems. In "Suffering the cold," for example, he addressed the tragedy of famine brought on by an exceptional cold snap, and noted: "Tigers and panthers are

---

14 See http://ctext.org/shuo-wen-jie-zi, *juan* 14, #8849. For further classical references, see https://baike.baidu.com/item/%E8%9B%9F/3592315 (accessed 1 April 2021).
15 See the reproduction of the text at https://zh.m.wikisource.org/wiki/%E6%98%AD%E6%98%8E%E6%96%87%E9%81%B8/%E5%8D%B74#%E8%9C%80%E9%83%BD%E8%B3%A6.
16 See the references in Morohashi Tetsuji, et alia, *Daikanwa jiten* (Tokyo: Taishūgen shoten, 1957–60), 10:33009, and Lo Zhufeng, et alia, *Hanyu dacidian* (Shanghai: Hanyu dacidian chubanshe, 1990–93), 8:893.
17 It is interesting that the elders used this term, which implies something beneficent, rather than *gui*, which is usually used in reference to evil. Exaltation of demonic beasts as objects of worship, and thereby pacification, was central to religious expression at least through the Tang.
18 Although separated today between Guangdong and Fujian, in the Tang Chaozhou and Quanzhou were both part of one large administrative region. Today Chaozhou is better known as Swatow, its local dialectical name.

motionless in their lairs/And even the *jiaochi* die in their secret depths." Or in "Dragons move about," a poem that remarked on the aftereffects of a major storm: "The *jiao* dragons move about in the dark of night."

Although deeply inscribed in the mythology of traditional Sinitic culture, this was not a welcome beast. Indeed, as the elders of Yongzhou affirmed, it was be dangerous. In this vein, Li Shizhen (1518–1593), author of the sixteenth-century *Bencao gangmu*, the *materia medica* that remains a standard reference for all Chinese flora and fauna, lumped the *jiao* in with dragons (*long*); in fact, like Han Yu he called the beast the "*jiao* dragon" (*jiaolong*).[19] Like the dragon, the *jiao* was a water beast. But where the dragon was viewed as irascible but ultimately beneficent, the *jiao* was not; Li explicitly asserted "its essence is poisonous" and added that to eat it was to fall ill. It was viewed, moreover, as a destructive beast that savaged river banks and broke dikes, causing catastrophic flooding.

Of course, knowing that the *jiao* is "a kind of dragon" only begs a further question: What is a dragon? And that, it turns out, is not so simple. Compare a dragon to a snake—after all, they are very much of the same order. Both are scaly; both are reviled. But there is critical difference: a snake is real. Whether, as in English, one calls it "snake," the Tamil *pāmpu*, the Latin *anguis*, or the Chinese *she*, we know we are only using different words to talk of the same thing, a real creature that occurs widely in the natural world for which almost all cultures have a parallel word. "Dragon," however, is a more complex concept because it is mythical, and myth is culturally dependent.[20] To begin with, "dragon" is an English word. Deriving from the Greek *drakos*, it refers to a fairly specialized manifestation of a far-larger concept: the four-limbed, scaly, commonly winged and lizard-like beast that often lives under or beside water and which is one of the oldest, most universal, yet most variable figures in Eurasian folk culture. In European folk tradition, the dragon is predatory and evil, a fearsome, loathsome and virtually impregnable fire-breathing demon against which mankind must pit its wits. Most readers are probably familiar with European tales of dragon-slayers, notably the tale of George and the dragon or the far-more recently conceived Smaug of the *Lord of the Rings* novels. But European dragon mythology has a far deeper heritage. The Greeks and Romans told dragon tales: The Greeks spoke of Andromeda, who was to be eaten by the horrific "sea-monster" Ketos but was rescued by Perseus the

---

19 Li Shizhen, *Bencao gangmu* (Shanghai: Shangwu shuju, 1933 ed.), j.43, quoted in Wang Daochun and Jiang Taozhuan, *Bencao pinhui jingyao xuji*, supplement to Liu Wentai, *Bencao pinhui jingyao* (Shanghai: Renmin weisheng chubanshe, 1982 photo reprint of 1701 ed.), 7a:1a–1b.
20 For a very interesting discussion that bears on this whole paragraph but makes this specific point, see G.D. Hornblower, "Early Dragon Forms," *Man* 33 (May 1933): 79–87.

"dragon-slayer,"[21] and the Romans, in a tale with Greek roots, of the party of Apuleius, who while traveling in the wilds was hailed by a desperate old man who begged for help. A young member of the party went to his aid, only not to return; he was found as a *draco/drakos* ate him.[22] More remotely, the ancient Mesopotamians, from whom the whole corpus of dragon legends may have its origins, told of the battle between the god Tishpak and the seven-headed dragon, decorated palace walls with dragon images, and immortalized the sea-monster Tiamat in their mythology.[23] The *naga* of Indian folklore is often invoked as a South Asian variation on the common theme, although *naga* are far more benign than the nasty serpents of Mesopotamia and Europe.[24]

In fact, the farther east one looks, the more benign the dragon figure becomes. Except in the farthest east, where popular culture recognized two kinds of dragon: the beneficent yet irascible *long* that brings rain and is featured in countless folk tales, and the predatory and dangerous *jiao*. But why does the *jiao* enter the story of Wu Xing? Although the retention dam for which he is credited disappeared long ago, the diversion of water from the Yanshou Creek into the network of canals that both irrigate and drain the Plain of Emerging Transformation remains a critical and very real piece of local infrastructure (see Map 2.2). The *jiao*, in contrast, is mythological; it does not exist. How do they fit together?

To answer that, let us return to Han Yu. Chaozhou was not the only place where Han found evidence of the *jiao*. Ouyang Zhan, a native of Quanzhou in southern Fujian that was adjacent to Chaozhou, had been his classmate in the imperial examinations.[25] Through Ouyang, Han Yu was introduced to the traditions of southern Fujian and wrote of *jiao* there as well:

> South of Quanzhou there is a mountain whose peaks stand up vertically. Below is a lake of over ten *mou* (ca. one-half acre), the depths of

---

21 The dragon-imagery is readily apparent in a Roman fresco of the first century BCE; see https://www.metmuseum.org/art/collection/search/250945 (accessed 1 April 2021).
22 On Apuleius, see Alex Scobie, "An Ancient Greek Drakos-Tale in Apuleius' *Metamorphoses* VIII, 19-21," *Journal of American Folklore* 90 (1977): 339–43.
23 Theodore Lewis, "*CT* 1333-34 and Ezekiel 32: Lion-Dragon Myths," *Journal of the American Oriental Society* 116, no. 1 (1996): 28–47, and Hornblower, "Early Dragon Forms." See also G. Rachel Levy, "The Oriental Origin of Herakles," *Journal of Hellenic Studies* 54, no. 1 (1954): 40–53, for reproductions of images from Sumerian and Akkadian artifacts.
24 "Encyclopedia Mythica," at http://www.pantheon.org/articles/n/nagas.html (accessed 26 December 2007).
25 Han Yu and Ouyang Zhan had passed the imperial examinations together in 792. Throughout the era of the examinations this constituted one of the deepest bonds between men, on a par with blood relationship. Illustratively, Han Yu wrote Ouyang's eulogy.

which cannot be guessed. There was a *jiao* that had caused the people great suffering. If people approached [the lake] by mistake, or if a horse or cow came for a drink, they usually were eaten. The people of Quanzhou had suffered thus for years. For this reason those who lived near the mountain had taken their wives and children elsewhere in order to escape the beast's horror.

Han's tale continues that one night in 810—surprisingly close in time to the tale of Wu Xing—there was a terrible commotion from within the mountain; it was so great that man and beast all hid in fear. When morning came the intrepid stepped out to see what had happened, and they found the mountain smashed to bits; the detritus had filled the lake, the land was leveled and all around was the red and black blood of the *jiaochi*. On the surrounding rocks nineteen characters had been inscribed in a style that was ancient and indecipherable; no one could read them. But thereafter the people were spared any more of the monster's depredations and the land returned to prosperity.[26]

Han's tale, in fact, links very directly to a real historical phenomenon. On a cliff-face overlooking a stream in the mountainous interior of Hua'an district (Zhangzhou) nineteen images of uncertain origin are inscribed. For many centuries they were known to the local people as the "immortals' inscription," an ancient and undecipherable inscription left by the Daoist divinities who had brought about the destruction of the *jiao*. Modern scholarship has concluded the images are Neolithic petroglyphs, not the undecipherable record of Daoist divinities, but there is little agreement on what, if anything, they seek to represent beyond highly stylized human figures (see Ill. 2.1).[27]

The question remains what, if anything, the *jiao* represented. Again, it is Han Yu who provides the answer. The saltwater crocodile (*Crocodylus porosus*), a real beast that is big enough to take down cattle and is well known to attack humans, historically could be found skulking in the marshes that characterized China's southern coast—the very marshes that Wu Xing was seeking to drain. Han lamented the curse of the crocodile, both in poetry and prose. For example, in a poem titled *The Supervisor of the Rapids*, a lamentation he wrote while on the last leg of his journey to exile in Chaozhou, he talked of his exile with the official, his traveling companion. After ascertaining Han's exile, the

---

26 Zhang Du, *Xuanshi zhi* (Siku quanshu electronic version; hereafter ESKQS) 5:12b–13b and *Taiping guangji* (ESKQS ed.) 392:1a–b.
27 See Zhu Weigan, *Fujian shigao* (Fuzhou: Fujian jiaoyu chubanshe, 1984), vol. 1:11–12; and the more contemporary analysis of Xu Xiaowang, *Fujian tongshi* (Fuzhou: Fujian renmin chubanshe, 2006), vol. 1:99.

Ill. 2.1 Zhangzhou Hua'an District cliff inscription. Source: https://kknews.cc/zh-my/culture/3obe258.html (accessed 2 April 2021).

clerk replied in language that must remind us of Liu Zongyuan's description of the *jiao*:

> There is a prefecture, its name is Chaozhou,
> Its loathsome waters are poisoned with miasmas.
> Thunder and lightning rumble and flash incessantly.
> The crocodiles are larger than boats,
> Their teeth and eyes cause us terror and death.[28]

Among Han's most intriguing texts from his exile is his *Offering to the Crocodile*, in which he ordered all the beasts to leave Chaozhou after receiving his sacrifice:

> Crocodiles, you may not live in this place with me. As prefect I have received the command of the Son of Heaven, which is to protect this land and provide order for these people. And you bug-eyed crocodiles do not bring peace to the streams and ponds. You eat the people and their cattle, bears, hogs, deer, and roebuck, all to fatten your bodies and nourish your young. Should you resist me, in the struggle I will emerge

---

28 This poem is also translated by Edward Schafer; see *The Vermilion Bird*, 217. For the full text, see "Long li," *Dongya tang changtai jizhu* (ESKQS ed.), 6:8a.

victorious. Though I may be stupid and weak, how could I bear to bow my head and surrender my heart to a crocodile.²⁹

Han's description and fear of the crocodile, which so echoes the prose he and others used to describe the *jiao*, suggests that in his mind they were the same animal, a link that goes back at least to the seventh-century scholar Li Chunfeng, who wrote:

> I have heard that the people of Guangzhou say … [the crocodile] lays several hundred eggs on dry land with each pregnancy. When they hatch they become several dozen animals, including snakes, turtles, sea turtles or fish, reptiles, and *jiao*. … Their numinous spirit can engender thunder and lightning, wind and rain and is to be feared.³⁰

The link between the terrifyingly real crocodile and the mythical *jiao* is finalized in an anonymous inscription from Quanzhou that addressed the events of 810 recorded by Han Yu, as mentioned above. This states quite explicitly that the beast that inhabited the pond, descried by Han Yu as a *jiao*, was in fact "a black and red crocodile celestial lord that killed people and cattle."³¹

Today the coast of eastern Guangdong and Fujian is free of crocodiles, but in Han's time the saltwater marshes that lined the coast such as that which challenged Wu Xing offered ideal habitat for the saltwater crocodile.³² It was, in fact, projects such as Wu Xing's that drained the marshes that had given habitat to the beasts and thus rendered the coast unsuitable to them. And like all crocodilians, *C. porosus* wallows in the soft soils of marshes and river banks, where they nest and rely on the mud to maintain body temperature. The holes they create, however, can undermine banks and become very destructive. A crocodile nesting in the banks of Wu Xing's canals would truly be a

---

29 See Xie Weixin, *Gujin hebi shilei beiyao bieji* (ESKQS ed.), 86:7a–b.
30 Quoted in Yang Shen, *Yiyu tu zanjian* (ESKQS ed.), 1:28 a–b.
31 See "Lei zhuan," in *Fujian jinshi zhi*, "shi"; in *Comprehensive Records of Fujian*, compiled by the Fujian Tongji Editorial Committee (Taipei: Datong shuju, 1968), 2:16a–b.
32 This point has been made by Jinzhong Fu, "Conservation, Management and Farming of Crocodiles in China," Proceedings of the 2nd Regional Meeting (Eastern Asia, Oceania, Australasia) of the Crocodile Specialist Group of the Species Survival Commission of IUCN—The World Conservation Union convened at Darwin, Northern Territory, Australia, 12 to 19 March 1993 (accessed at http://www.iucncsg.org/365_docs/attachments/protarea/Reg%20-17d4a33d.pdf, 27 November 2017). More recently, He Xin has made a similar point, emphasizing the impact of human activity on the species; see *Zhushen de qiyuan, di er juan: lun long yu feng de dongwuxue yuanli* (Beijing: Zhongguo minzhu fazhi, 2009), chapter 3, "Shen long de zhixiang."

disaster. There can be no doubt that the *jiao* that caused so much damage to Wu Xing's project was in fact a crocodile. Given its reputation for eating large animals, the beast almost surely was *C. porosus*.

There are many questions that lie behind this story, from the elementary issue of what drove Wu Xing to organize such an ambitious project to the far more complicated question of why the narrative identified the destructive crocodile as a mythical *jiao*. These are the immediate questions we shall engage through the following pages as we assess the transformation of southern China from an alien frontier into the core of the empire, the presentist concern, and ask if that transformation had to be, the unstated teleological premise.

Chapter 3

SOME BACKGROUND

Recall a point from the opening chapter: The land we call China was not always Chinese. In fact, in a very real sense for many eons, when the world of Sinitic culture was defined by the Central Plain, no one was Chinese, a term I shall argue that only gains real meaning in the last millennium. Through most of the first millennium BCE, the people of the Central Plain, the Yellow River flood plain where classical Sinitic culture emerged, called their land "the courts (or kingdoms, i.e., *guo*) in the center," or *Zhongguo*. As explained in Chapter 1, this was both a political and cultural term, referencing a large and diverse realm across the Plain that shared several defining attributes, most notably a parallel, if not entirely identical, orthography through which the literate elite shared a common body of classical texts. What it did not mean then, as it has come to mean only in recent times, is China. A range of terms were used instead by the people of the Sinitic world to refer to their homeland; as the Sinitic world gained definition, *Zhongguo* instead defined the geophysical realm of Sinitic culture, and Sinitic culture defined civilization.[1]

These several "courts in the center" shared an academic culture that fostered a degree of commonality even as they remained politically and linguistically disunited. This was much like the diverse courts and cultures of late medieval Europe, where a common cultural discourse built on Latin, the shared language of the literate elite, and the broadly shared premises of Christianity provided a common identity even as they simultaneously maintained regionalized and localized political and colloquial identity. Like medieval Europe, the Central Plain through the first millennium BCE remained

---

1 Ironically, China is not even derived from a Chinese word. Merchants in West and South Asia referred to a semi-mythologized land that lay beyond the mountains far to the east as *sina*, or *china*, a term they derived from *Qin* (pronounced "chin"), the name of the westernmost kingdom (or *guo*) of the Sinitic world. As the Roman empire developed trade links, especially with the west coast of the Indian subcontinent, the term and the mythology associated with it migrated west where it became the default term of reference to that far-off and extensively mythologized land.

a fractious and restricted realm. The goal of this chapter is to illustrate the cultural transformation from Sinitic toward one that was to become China, from a world that was both geographically and culturally constrained to one that was geographically vast and culturally diverse. That is, how did Sinitic China become holistic China?

As a coherent and shared Sinitic culture emerged out of the ancient regional cultures of the Central Plain, beyond the "courts in the center" was a complex world of many divergent and often very local peoples and cultures. In what follows I specifically will explore what we can say about the people who lived along the coast of that region we today call Fujian, concentrating on the times before Wu Xing's Distributed Blessings Retention Dam. What transpired there, however, should be understood as a microcosm of what transpired broadly across the lands south of the Central Plain through the first millennium CE.

From north to south the Fujian coast divides into four river basins:

- the Min River basin of the north, draining by far the largest area and defined by the modern city of Fuzhou;
- the Mulan River basin, centered on the modern city of Putian and the irrigation networks that drained the lower reaches of the river, including the Distributed Blessings network;
- the Jin River basin of the upper south, by which maritime ships for centuries accessed the port of Quanzhou that Marco Polo, who visited in the later thirteenth century, called the greatest port in the world; and
- the Jiulong River basin of the deeper south, adjacent to modern Guangdong province and defined by modern Zhangzhou.[2]

In the deeper past much of the Fujian coastline, as well as the lower course of these rivers as each broached the mountainous interior out to the flat coastal plain and the sea, was marshland. Each basin, moreover, is separated from the others by mountain ridges, which has led to a divergence of local cultures and dialects that persists even to the present. By far the largest, the Min River basin in the north, drains more than half of all Fujian. Through a common orientation along the upper reaches of the basin the several regions of the northern interior had access to the lower delta region and the open ocean. Nevertheless, as a result of geography and distinct histories the several regions of the interior had divergent and mutually unintelligible dialects.

---

2 There is one additional river network, the Ting River, which drains the southwest corner of Fujian. Because the Ting flows out of Fujian and through Chaozhou in adjacent Guangdong, I do not include it in this discussion.

Similarly, the three southern basins, which collectively drain the southern third of the region (*Min nan*[3]) all have dialectical distinctions as well. Although all three are considered variations on southern Min dialect, that of the Mulan basin (Putian) is especially distinct while those of the Jin and Jiulong basins are close enough that speakers of each can understand the other, much as a native of Milan can pierce through the regionalisms of southern Italy to understand someone from Naples or a native of Frankfurt can understand someone from Munich. Reflecting their dialectical traditions, each region has distinct culinary and cultural traditions, including distinct deities that we shall discuss below, that further define them separately. Thus, far from being an integrated whole, Fujian has always been a fractured world of regionalisms. As the modern scholar Xu Xiaowang has summarized it, "There was little flat land that was suitable for human settlement. Even where there were such suitable places, they were separated by distance and going back and forth was not easy."[4]

There are some characteristics, however, that have provided commonality across all four regions and between the Fujian coast and cultures in the Yangtze basin further north since the ancient past. The nearly universal cultivation of rice was among the most important. Evidence suggests that for millennia hunter–gatherers throughout the south had collected wild rice kernels. Undomesticated wild rice comes in numerous varieties that will grow in a range of conditions, but the most productive are marsh grasses that prosper with wet roots. Riziculture, the purposeful cultivation of rice, evolved in the central and lower Yangtze River basin through the middle of the first deca-millennium BCE. Excavations have found evidence of paddy fields, diked fields that can alternately be flooded and drained and so mimic marshland conditions, notably at the Hemudu site on the South shore of Hangzhou Bay dating ca. 5,000 BP. Mastering the technology of paddy construction was an important innovation in the successful domestication of rice.

The spread of riziculture to the emergent cultures of Fujian occurred much later than in the Hangzhou Bay region and the Yangtze basin, as recently explained by Zhang Chi and Hong Xiaochun (Hung Hsiao-ch'un):

[S]ubsistence strategies in Lingnan-Fujian [i.e., the South and southeast coasts] and southwest China after the early Neolithic continued with a heavy emphasis on fishing and hunting. The first direct evidence

---

3 "Min" is a classical name for the greater Fujian region. In most applications, however, it refers only to the Min River's drainage basin. The term *Min nan*, which in common discourse for centuries has meant southern Fujian, literally means "south of the Min River."
4 Xu, *Fujian tongshi*, vol. 1, 2.

for farming appeared only in the late phase of the late Neolithic, after 3500 B.C., apparently as a result of farming dispersal from the Yangtze basin.[5]

The earliest evidence of riziculture in the river basins of Fujian is limited to the Min River basin, where the influence of the cultures surrounding Hangzhou Bay that were leading the way was most pronounced. As presently understood, riziculture, including the construction of paddy, dispersed from the Neolithic cultures around the Hangzhou Bay to the Tanshishan culture of northern Fujian by 3,000–4,000 BP. As explained, however, the cultures of the southern basins were cut off from those of the Min River basin both by physical separation as well as cultural and linguistic distinctions. The inhabitants of these basins continued to focus on gathering the wild but rich resources of the coastal marshes and inland forests. Because cropping was a secondary focus, rather than develop the labor-intensive paddy that were spreading through the lower reaches of the Min River basin they relied on swidden, or "slash-and-burn," agriculture. Areas cleared by burning existing vegetation are enriched by the ash and can initially produce bountiful harvests, but the fertility of the soil is quickly exhausted; without ongoing fertilization "slash-and-burn" clearings must be abandoned after a short number of crop cycles and left to a slow process of natural refertilization. Because swidden agriculture is therefore impermanent, a corollary is a limit on the development of permanent village settlement. This in turn inhibited the development of skills that are the product of fixed workshops such as metallurgy and pottery making. In the central and southern basins these skills indeed lagged behind those of the Min River basin and especially behind other regions further north on the shores of the Hangzhou Bay as well as along the Yangtze River.[6] Thus in many respects the culture and economy of the coastal regions south of the Min River basin remained comparatively undeveloped. The exception was in the exploitation of the coastal marsh and off-shore waters.

The Fujian coast south of the Min River alternates between peninsular headlands and scalloped bays. The coastal waters remain shallow almost everywhere but especially in the bays, where even today the reclamation of

---

5 Zhang Chi and Hsiao-Chun Hung, "The Neolithic of Southern China–Origin, Development, and Dispersal," *Asian Perspectives* 47, no. 2 (2008): 299–329. https://muse.jhu.edu/ (accessed 8 October 2018), quoting 312.
6 See *Fujian Jinjiang liuyu kaogu diaocha yu yanjiu*, edited by Zheng Guozhen and the Fujian Jinjiang liuyu kaogu diaocha yuan (Beijing: Kexue chubanshe, 2010).

new land by draining the coastal fringe is an ongoing process.[7] These waters were an essential resource for the ancient people, as is apparent from the several Neolithic shell mounds found along the coast. These have yielded a range of marine resources, including shellfish and the bones of marine species.[8] While the large quantities of shellfish would have been collected in the tidal marshes and adjacent shallow waters that were easy to access, larger species such as shark, remains of which are also plentiful, required open water skills, which raises the further question of nautical technology. Taiwanese anthropologist Ling Shun-sheng has suggested the Neolithic cultures of the southeast coast used bamboo rafts such as those still used in the coastal estuaries of Fujian and Taiwan (see Ill. 5.1), a suggestion that is now widely shared among scholars.[9] Consisting of bamboo poles lashed together with natural fibers, these craft are simple to build, and certainly within the skill set of the Neolithic cultures. At the same time, they are remarkably seaworthy; when equipped with steering oar and outrigger they can even manage the waters of the open ocean. In fact, the widely shared assumption in scholarship today is that having first used such craft to cross the Taiwan Strait and occupy that island as much as 30,000 BP, it was descendants of those settlers who used the same craft to further settle the Philippines and the islands of the Southwest and Central Pacific.

We are no doubt correct to assume, therefore, that the early inhabitants of the coast and off-shore islands were generally comfortable on the water. Indeed, writing of the descendants of survivors of a fifth-century rebellion who had found refuge on the Fujian coast, a tenth-century text that we shall return to later tells us: "The barbarian households of [Quanzhou] prefecture are known as the 'floating boat people.'"[10] The description suggests that some

---

[7] See, for example, the nautical chart BA 1723, "Xinghua wan and approaches," at https://www.cairnscharts.com.au/products/ba1723 (accessed 17 October 2018).
[8] Peter Bellwood, *Pre-History of the Indo-Malaysian Archipelago* (Sidney: ANU Press, 1977), 213, with further citations. See also Fujian Provincial Museum and the Anthropology Department of Harvard University, "An Archaeological Investigation of the Damaoshan Site, Fujian Province," *Chinese Archaeology* 4 (2004): 76–81.
[9] Ling Shun-sheng, "Formosan Sea-Going Raft and its Origin in Ancient China," in *A Study of the Raft, Outrigger, Double, and Deck Canoes of Ancient China, the Pacific and the Indian Oceans* (Taipei: Academic Sinica Institute of Ethnology, 1970), 77–99; see also Barry V. Rolett, Zhuo Zheng, and Yuanfu Yue, "Holocene Sea-Level Change and the Emergence of Neolithic Seafaring in the Fuzhou Basin (Fujian, China)," *Quaternary Science Reviews* 30, no. 7–8 (2011): 788–97.
[10] Yue Shi, *Taiping huanyu ji* (Taipei: Wenhai chubanshe, 1962 reprint of 1803 ed.; henceforth TPHYJ), 102:2b.

36 A NARRATIVE OF CULTURAL ENCOUNTER IN SOUTHERN CHINA

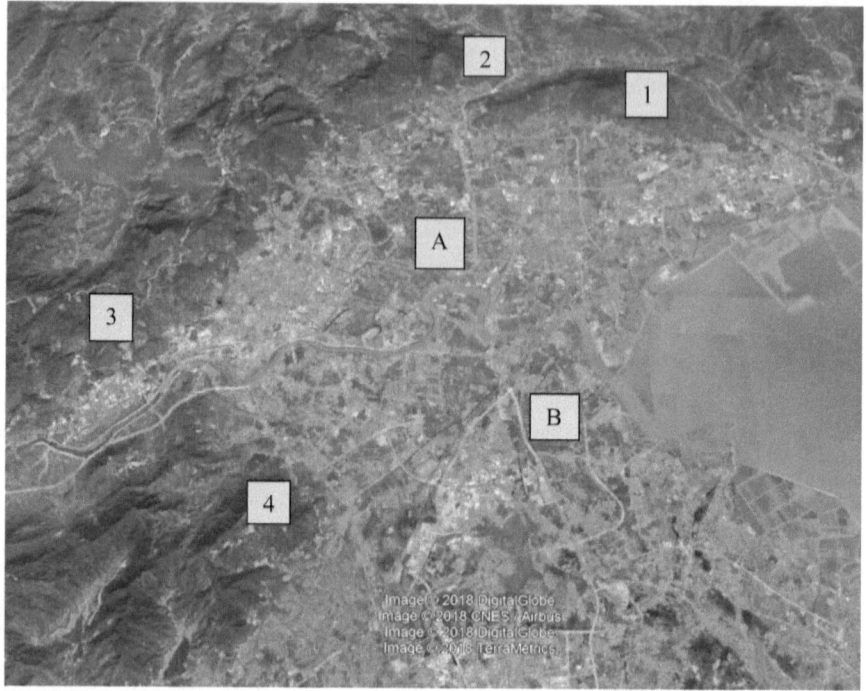

Map 3.1 Putian, showing the approximate areas of the northern and southern irrigation networks and Neolithic settlement sites. Source: Google Earth.
A: Irrigation network of the Distributed Blessings Retention Dam (north of Mulan River). B: Irrigation network of the Mulan River Retention Dam (south of Mulan River) 1. Jiangkou District, 2. Wutang District, 3. Huating District and 4. Lingchuan District.

may have even lived on their boats, as the "boat people" known as the *Dan* do today along the southeast and south coast.

Of course, not everyone lived permanently on the water. Evidence of dry land settlements, for example, has also been found in the hills that overlooked Wu Xing's reclamation project. Revealingly, the sites predominantly lie on the edge of the uplands on the slopes facing the open sea where they are beyond the reach of tides (see Map 3.1). These sites conveniently provide ready access both to the fauna and flora of the dry interior as well as the products of the marsh and the sea. As a summary of the excavations of Neolithic sites in Lingchuan District (Map 3.1, #4) explains:

> Long ago there were verdant forests on the mountains where wild animals came and went. In the seas all kinds of fish were abundant. It was an environment blessed by nature that gave the people of ancient times an exceptional quality of life. They could go into the mountains to hunt

the wild animals or down to the sea where they could collect the myriad creatures.[11]

These are all material issues: technology, agriculture and how the ancient inhabitants of the southeast coast lived. What did they believe about the world in which they lived? Theirs was a world in close contact with nature. Totemic images and associated legends of frogs, tadpoles and fish combine with popular traditions from across the region to point to a benign side of nature. Like so many in the ancient world, however, they also encountered a world that was full of threat. When they ventured out to sea there were storms and unexplained disappearances. The hills where they gathered plants and hunted animals also harbored venomous snakes, such as cobra; constrictors, such as pythons; destructive animals, such as elephants; and predatory animals, such as tigers. And like their peers across that ancient world, they sought to appease the threats through veneration. In recent years, for example, several rock carvings of threatening snakes have been identified in the hills behind the coastal plain. Perhaps the most intriguing is a carving of a large snake that is apparently attacking something (see Ill. 3.1), perhaps a granary. Some suggest that the distinct shape under the snake represents a nest; a similar motif of juvenile snakes appears in other stone engravings from the same area.[12]

Regardless of the precise interpretation, it is apparent that the carving illustrates a fear of snakes, a fear that manifests as well in folk tradition. We find, for example, in *In Search of the Supernatural* (Soushen ji), a compilation of folk tales originally compiled in the fourth century with many later additions, the tale of a predatory snake "eighty or ninety feet in length and with a girth more than ten arm spans wide" that lived in the hinterland of the Min River basin in northern Fujian. It had killed officials and elders and had been offered sacrifices of cattle and sheep, "all to no avail." Eventually the snake demanded an annual sacrifice of a virgin girl, which year by year for nine years the people provided. The tenth girl, however, a paragon of virtue, the youngest of six children who offered herself so her parents would not have to bear the burden of raising her, instead tricked the snake and killed it.[13]

---

11 "Lingchuan zhen sanci faxian xinshiqi shidai shiqi," at https://kknews.cc/culture/zmzggll.html (accessed 23 October 2018).
12 See, for example, http://ouyangxijun.blog.sohu.com/157918206.html (accessed November 2020).
13 Gan Bao, *In Search of the Supernatural: The Written Record*, translated by Kenneth DeWoskin and J.I. Crump (Stanford: Stanford University Press, 1996), 230–31. Lest one wonders at the apparent contradiction between her killing the snake, and so surviving,

Ill. 3.1 Caozi Mountain snake petroglyph (with enhancement). Source: http://ouyangxijun.blog.sohu.com/157918206.html (accessed 31 October 2018).

Another tale, of uncertain origin but also from the Min River hinterland, tells of the battle between the Lady Linshui and the "white serpent." Like the snake of the preceding tale, this snake was also massive and predatory; it also was ultimately killed by a young woman.[14] These are not the tales of Sinitic culture. Both reflect the pre-Sinitic indigenous tradition.

A further variant on the snake motif is the cult of the Lord Master of the (Daoist) Law (*Fazhu gong*), a cult that even today remains widespread through the inland prefectures of Fujian as well as in Taiwan. Cult tradition identifies the Lord as a Daoist master surnamed Zhang and places him in the eleventh century. Master Zhang is alleged to have sworn an oath with two colleagues to defeat a predatory snake demon that "for a thousand years" had terrorized the people of Yongchun, a mountainous district in the Quanzhou interior that is very much a part of the highland corridor where the two preceding narratives are located.[15] Following his defeat of the snake Master Zhang immediately became a celestial being.

---

and her willing self-sacrifice in order to spare her parents, in appreciation the local lord married the girl and ennobled her parents. All was well!
14 BMTZ, 58:373.
15 Xu Xiaowang, *Fujian minjian xinyang yuanliu* (Fuzhou: Fujian jiaoyu chubanshe, 1993), 41. See also https://religion.moi.gov.tw/Knowledge/Content?ci=2&cid=287 (accessed 4 November 2018).

The eleventh century was a time when the Sinitic world was experiencing a major cultural transformation. This is most commonly identified with the reformist ideology known as Neo-Confucianism, but the upheaval extended deeply into all cultural spheres, including Daoism which experienced major liturgical innovations. Many scholars have argued as well that this was a fertile time in the formulation of popular cult traditions, including the emergence of new deities and redefinition of old ones.[16] Master Zhang is illustrative. In addition to his confrontation with the snake demon, his cult teaches that he preached throughout the upland regions of Fuzhou and Quanzhou, where he developed a reputation for saintliness as he summoned rain in the face of drought and repelled plague demons. Although the three traditions connected to Master Zhang: defeating the snake, confronting plague demons and praying to the rain gods, are fused into a single cult, they appear to have had separate origins. It is certainly plausible that Master Zhang may have existed, that he was inspired by innovations in Daoism to preach through the upland regions of Fujian. This was a region where the population included both *de classé* Sinitic immigrants and remnant survivors of the indigenous people, among whom belief in the myriad cult deities, both demonic and benign, was likely to have remained strong in the face of a growing academic secularism.[17] His confrontation with the snake demon of Yongchun, however, almost surely draws on the ancient indigenous snake narratives and perhaps refers to the earliest layer of the cult. Like the tale from *In Search of the Supernatural* and that of the Lady Linshui, the narrative of the snake certainly derives from a much older indigenous tradition. The cult that emerged in the Song, it appears, was an amalgamation of that ancient indigenous tradition with the more recent influence of Sinitic culture.

In a similar vein, the *Comprehensive Record of the Eight Regions of Fujian* (BaMin tongzhi), a provincial gazetteer compiled late in the fifteenth century, addresses Dawu Mountain, which overlooks the sea near the Zhangzhou border with Quanzhou: "The Altar to the Lady of Dawu is on this mountain. An inscription records: 'When as yet there was no living person in Min [i.e., Fujian], the goddess cleared the land so people could settle.'"[18] Her physical

---

16 See, for example, Xu, *Minjian xinyang*, Valerie Hansen, *Changing Gods in Medieval China. 1127–1276* (Princeton: Princeton University Press, 1990), and Hugh R. Clark, "What Makes a Chinese God? or What Makes a God Chinese?," in *Imperial China and Its Southern Neighbors* (Singapore: Institute for Southeast Asian Studies, 2015), 111–39.
17 See, for example, Richard von Glahn, *The Sinister Way: The Divine and the Demonic in Chinese Religious Culture* (Berkeley: University of California Press, 2004).
18 *BaMin tongzhi* (Fuzhou: Fujian renmin, 1989 ed.), 8:146; see also *QuanTang wen* 513, accessed through ctext.org (28 October 2018).

link to the sea suggests that the Lady of Dawu was more than just the goddess of the land, for the sea was a place of danger. Storms were one such, but so were the creatures that live in the sea. As has been mentioned earlier, shark bones are among the remains found in Neolithic shell mounds, but among predatory animals of the sea sharks were not alone. As has been discussed in Chapter 2, the coast was plagued by crocodiles. Because of man's adaptation of the coast to economic needs, an issue we shall return to in greater depth in Chapter 5, it has been many years since the saltwater crocodile was a regular danger in the coastal waters and estuaries of the Fujian coast. However, an eighteenth-century gazetteer recalls that as late as 1527 Wu Kai, when serving as magistrate in eastern Guangdong province adjacent to Fujian's southern border, banished crocodiles for the harm they were causing the people, echoing Han Yu's edict of nearly a millennium earlier mentioned previously and indicating that they remained a concern.[19]

Given the tradition of venerating dangerous terrestrial animals as a way of appeasing them, we might expect to see something similar with dangerous marine animals, and in fact we do. From the beginning of the Sinitic record crocodiles were equated with *jiao* which removed them from the realm of secular reality into the mythical and the numinous. This has been introduced previously, but it is emphasized in a passage from the *Garden of Stories* (Shuo yuan), a compilation of anecdotes compiled in the Former Han period (206 BCE–8 CE). An envoy from the Yue kingdom, addressing a prince of the very early Han, observed of his land:

> The *jiao* dragons contested the land with us. Thus, we have cut our hair and tattooed our bodies so that we fully resemble the dragons.[20]

In a similar vein, an anecdote in the *Record of the Grand Historian* (Shi ji) recounts that in 210 BCE the founding emperor of the Qin dynasty (221–209 BCE) was crossing the Yangtze delta region as he toured his empire when he encountered Xu Shi, a "man of arts" (*fangshi*), a proto-Daoist movement that emphasized magic. Xu lamented that for years he had tried to gather "sacred medicine" from the sea but had routinely suffered harm from sharks and had thus failed. That night the emperor dreamed that he did battle with a "sea deity" shaped like a man. Puzzled, he asked his courtiers about it, and one informed him: "One cannot see a sea deity, so instead one sees a large fish or

---

19 *(Qianlong) Jinjiang xianzhi* j.10:51b.
20 Liu Xiang, *Shuo yuan* 12, "Feng shi," anecdote #11, at https://ctext.org/shuo-yuan/feng-shi/zh (accessed 2 November 2018).

a *jiao* dragon. Now, because you offered prayers as a caution you have exorcised this bad spirit and can access the good spirits."[21]

Jiao, in short, were among the myriad numinous creatures that were believed to inhabit the shores and shallows of the southeast coast. Like snakes, they were a source of danger, a "bad spirit." The *jiao* that attacked the dikes of Wu Xing's reclamation project so many centuries later was not exactly fictitious; as explained in the preceding chapter, it was a crocodile. But by labelling it a mythical *jiao*, the tale places the crocodile in the same pantheon of dangerous spirits as the mythologized snake. To the ancient peoples of the southeast coast, and indeed to the ancient peoples across the South, the natural world was filled with dangers. Survival required care, including sacrificial appeasement.

This was the world Wu Xing set out to transform. As much as we know about his project, however, we know very little about the man himself. Who was he? Almost nothing survives to answer that question. There is no reliable record of his ancestry, nor of when his patriline might have arrived in the Mulan Valley.[22] In the absence of any more contemporary records we must take it on faith, in fact, that the man himself even existed, that he was not simply a cultural projection akin to legendary figures such as Paul Bunyan. Presuming his reality, for there is no reason to doubt it other than the absence of contemporary information, his ability to marshal the labor his project required when the Sinitic immigrant population was growing strongly suggests he too was ethnically Sinitic, although even that can never be conclusively determined.

Regardless, at a time when ethnicity in the region remained confused and shifting, when the intruding Sinitic immigrants challenged the heritage of the pre-Sinitic indigenes, Wu Xing must have emerged among the most powerful figures in the new ethno-cultural alignment. At such a chronological distance as to be legitimately suspect, the seventeenth-century *Minshu* comments that "he used his wealth to be a hero [or 'champion'] in his community," while the nineteenth-century Putian gazetteer—written more than a full millennium removed from Wu Xing and his project and so further compromised by its added distance from the event—noted that "he used his family wealth to

---

21 Sima Qian, *Shi ji* 6, "Qin Shihuang benji," anecdote #45, at https://ctext.org/shiji/qin-shi-huang-ben-ji/zh (accessed 18 December 2018).
22 A variety of modern web sites assert that Wu had relocated from Quanzhou to Putian, although how his kin had arrived in Quanzhou is not noted, nor do these sites offer any proof to support their assertion. It is likely the claim may be based on a Wu clan genealogy, but that too is not mentioned.

construct the weir."²³ Shy any more contemporary reference, neither source can be taken as authoritative, yet both are no doubt in some sense correct for Wu Xing clearly had the authority and/or influence to mobilize the labor and wealth his project required. Despite the absence of any more contemporary records, in other words, this all argues that Wu Xing was both wealthy and influential, and most likely a major landowner, the most plausible source of such wealth at that time.

There is one point, however, on which Wu Xing apparently had fully committed to the Sinitic cultural model: He believed in the importance, if not indeed the primacy, of agriculture among available economic pursuits. His project was not intended to improve the harvest of fish or game; it was an agricultural project pure and simple that in fact made the pursuit of marine resources more difficult. He moreover was prepared to expend considerable capital on realizing it. Just as cutting down the forests of New England or breaking the prairie sods of Kansas as the agriculturally intensive European immigrants displaced the extensive economies of the indigenous cultures on the American frontier was as much a cultural as an economic statement, so Wu Xing's conversion of the unproductive marshes of the Plain of Emerging Transformation into some of the Sinitic world's most bounteous agricultural lands was as much a rejection of the economy and culture of the pre-Sinitic inhabitants as it was a positive economic program.

---

23 He Qiaoyuan, *Minshu* (Fuzhou: Fujian renmin, 1995) 24:578 and *(Guangxu) Putian xianzhi*, compiled by Song Ruolin et al. (Taipei: Chengwen shuju chubanshe, 1968 reprint of 1879 ed.), 27:1a.

Chapter 4

THE SINITIC ENCOUNTER AND WU XING

Although the cultural and demographic heritage of the southern river basins was distinct from that of the Central Plain and Yellow River basin, throughout the first millennium CE the South was undergoing an historic transformation as both cultural and demographic interaction with the Plain intensified. Although it began even before the Han dynasty, this interaction gained momentum after the early first millennium disaster connected with the usurpation of Wang Mang (45 BCE–23 CE), who briefly reigned as emperor of the Xin dynasty (r. 9–23 CE).[1]

Even before Wang's usurpation and interregnum, emigrants from the North had trickled into the South. Much like the emigrants who made their way to North America many centuries later in search of security and new opportunities, they had been pushed by the increasingly oppressive exactions of northern landlords and pulled by the seductive promise of agricultural bounty. Also like those European migrants, these migrants were unprepared to recognize the indigenous folk they encountered as equally, or even fully, human. Thus as these migrants, following river valleys, found their way to the Yangtze basin, like those European migrants who had undertaken similarly perilous journeys, they presumed the land was theirs to take. And so the migration proceeded, via the north-flowing tributaries of the great river that had their sources in the southern mountains, all the way to the great southern port city known then as Panyu and more recently as Guangzhou (what European traders many centuries later called Canton, based on how they

---

1 Traditional Chinese historiography divides the Han into two eras. The roughly two centuries before Wang Mang's usurpation (206 BCE–9 CE) are referred to as either the "Former" or "Western" Han, and the roughly equal time after (23–220 CE) as the "Latter" or "Eastern" Han. The designations "West" and "East" are based on the relative location of the imperial court.

heard the regional pronunciation of Guangdong, the name of the province of which Panyu or Guangzhou has long been the capital).

Throughout the first millennium CE, these migrants lived alongside the indigenous peoples, sometimes peacefully but often not so. Whatever the nature of their interaction, however, gradually the cultures of both were transformed. Though some of the migrants came with backgrounds rooted in the elite customs of the north, by far the majority were common folk. Primarily they were peasants to whom the customs of the elite were as alien as were those of the southern cultures with which they found themselves enmeshed. However, if the elites kept themselves apart from the indigenes, whom they regarded as uncivilized barbarians unworthy of their notice, to the common folk they were neighbors—no doubt often not only their rivals for the land, but also guides in how to live in the alien, and sometimes dangerous, environment of the South.

The interactions among these several cultural and demographic groups were complex. Consider the family of Wang Hong, among the most prominent courtiers under the Liu Song dynasty (420–79, not to be confused with the [Zhao] Song dynasty of the tenth–thirteenth centuries) that followed the Jin in the South. Although the new dynasty is noted for recruiting southerners into its bureaucracy and pushing forward an accommodation between North and South in the Yangtze basin, Wang claimed descent from one of the most illustrious families of the Central Plain. In keeping with the claimed origins, after generations of service to the Han dynasty, his great-grandfather had been Counselor-in-Chief (*chengxiang*), the highest civil position of the Jin dynasty court administration; whether this was before or after the court's relocation to the Yangtze basin is not stated.[2] Significantly, although they resided in Jiankang (Nanjing), neither Wang Hong, his patrilineal ancestors, nor his heirs throughout the era of division ever identified themselves as natives of the South; they were native to the Central Plain.

This stands in contrast to the family of Gu Yong (?–243) whose ancestors had settled in the city known today as Suzhou, located on the immensely fertile south shore of the Hangzhou Bay late in the Han dynasty. Here the indigenous southern culture already had a long history of technological sophistication and material prosperity, yet to Gu Yong they were barbarians. Gu served under the Wu kingdom (222–80), southernmost of the so-called Three Kingdoms that emerged out of the wreckage of the Han in the early third century. Like Wang Hong, he ultimately rose to Counselor-in-Chief.

---

2 See the biographies of Wang Xiang and Wang Lan in *Jin shu* (ESKQS ed.) j.33, and Wang Hong's biography in *Song shu* (ESKQS ed.), 42:11b–28a.

Also, like Wang Hong, Gu Yong was a southerner by birth, but his great-grandfather had served the Han as the prefect of Yinchuan located in modern Henan province on the northwestern perimeter of the Central Lands at the edge of the Gobi desert, about as far from the lush South as one could get.[3]

There is no record of why Gu's patriline had relocated to the South; it is likely that it was in connection with the troubles that afflicted the Han through its last decades, troubles that had prompted one of the early waves of migration toward the South. What we do know is that as a prefectural magistrate his great-grandfather had served the Han in a regionally powerful position, and that Gu Yong, having been born in a southern city and growing to adulthood under the southern Wu dynasty, rose to his empire's most powerful civil office. His links to the Han elite were no doubt a contributing factor to his own elite status.

In contrast to the prominent heritage of Wang Hong and Gu Yong, most Sinitic migrants came from families that had been socially marginal in their northern homes of origin. The vast majority lived and died as peasants; like the native southerners among whom they lived, they remain entirely anonymous. A small number, however, took advantage of the fluid nature of social hierarchy in the South to climb the social ladder to positions that have left a record. Whether their ancestors had had a northern background or were from the indigenous culture, they emerge in the records as a new southern elite that stood apart from the relocated northern elites such as Gu Yong.

For example, Tao Kan (259–334), the great-grandfather of the famous poet Tao Yuanming (365?–427), was born in Poyang in the central Yangtze basin. This was both culturally and spatially remote from the highly Sinicized courts that were based in Jiankang, in the lower reaches of the Yangtze basin. Sources tell us nothing about the origins of the family except that Kan was the son of a general who had served Wu, and that his mother was a native southerner. The family was apparently prominent among the regional elite of the central Yangtze valley, but this was an area of decidedly contested cultural heritage. In one oft-cited encounter, Tao Kan was even referred to by a scornful northerner as "the dog of Xi" (*Xi gou*), invoking a local indigenous, and so barbarian, group.[4]

It is impossible from such random strands of information to draw any firm conclusions about the ethnic background of Tao Kan's family, but that in itself is indicative. Men who could claim a link to the Han elites did so proudly, as

---

3 Chen Shou, *Sanguo zhi*, "Wu zhi" 7:8a, quoting the no longer extant "Annals of Wu" (*Wu lu*).
4 Liu Yiqing, *Shishuo xinyu*, 2b:5a.

Wang Hong and Gu Yong did. They were unlikely to choose to live far from the center of political power, deep in the heart of the indigenous South, nor were they likely to marry native southerners. As a general serving the Wu court, Tao Kan's father had gained a measure of regional social prominence; the stark divide between military and civil elites that characterized later times was as yet unrealized. What we know of his marriage, however, suggests that within the Sinitic world his position was marginal. Perhaps the Tao were *de classé* migrants who had managed to climb the military ladder, or perhaps they were of the indigenous non-Sinitic elite who had accommodated to the Sinitic power structure. Neither heritage offered an easy path to authority in the hierarchy of the Sinitic imperial order.

Not surprisingly, therefore, the Tao were suspect in the eyes of the heirs to Sinitic cultural orthodoxy. As a young man aspiring to greater things, however, Tao Kan went north to Luoyang, capital of the Western Jin dynasty. There he sought to meet with the great official Zhang Hua. Regarding Kan as a country bumpkin, Zhang initially refused to see him—it was he who dismissed Kan as a "dog of Xi." However, "When Zhang saw that Kan venerated the spirits [of his ancestors] without disrespect, he conversed with him and marveled," leading to a reconsideration and an appointment in Zhang's entourage. Having established himself thereby as sufficiently worthy, Kan became Zhang's protégé. Yet Zhang never saw him as fully civilized, proclaiming instead, "Henceforth this is our man for overseeing pacified peoples."[5] Zhang then assigned him to posts across the Farther South with titles such as "Commander of the Southern Man barbarians" and later as magistrate of Guangzhou, as the aforementioned Panyu was now known. Postings such as these only emphasized his cultural and social affinity with the uncivilized peoples he oversaw. After all, as the ancient saying noted, "one uses barbarians to control barbarians." Tao Kan may have been able to "venerate the spirits without disrespect," but whatever his family's origins, in the eyes of the northern elite he was always defined by the questionable standards of the South.

Finally, consider Hu Fan (372–433) and Luo Qisheng (no dates), brothers-in-law from Nanchang district.[6] Nanchang sat at the southern end of the Poyang Lake near the mouth of the Gan River, one of the several north-flowing tributaries of the Yangtze River. In later times the district became a prominent agricultural center, however, under the Jin dynasty it was a

---

5 *Shishuo xinyu* 1A:40b, commentary of Liu Xiaobiao.
6 The following is based on their respective biographies. On Hu Fan, see *Song shu* 50:1a–4b; on Luo Qisheng, see *Jin shu* 89:31b–33a.

garrison town beyond which the influence of the Sinitic culture that defined civilization was limited. Hu Fan's patrilineal ancestors at least through his grandfather had held mid-level military and civil positions under the Jin, but there is no suggestion that they had northern roots. Hu Fan was orphaned at a young age, which "interrupted his career," but he gained the attention of regionally powerful officials who promoted him to colleagues through whom he was appointed to a mid-level military post in the entourage of the governor of Jingzhou, like Nanchang a garrison town in the Yangtze basin adjacent to Sichuan. In the context of the place and time, Hu had married well; his brother-in-law Luo Xiansheng was in the entourage of the prefect of Jingzhou.

Luo's biography says he had been born poor, which led him to seek a post as an officer in the garrison in Linru (modern Fuzhou [Jiangxi]), placing him deep into the native south and further from the reach of Sinitic culture. From there he earned a series of promotions that also led to the entourage of the Jingzhou governor.

We know of these two men because later scholars deemed them worthy of biographies. However, unlike Wang Hong, Gu Yong or Tao Kan, all of whom came from families that were socially or politically significant, neither Hu Fan nor Luo Qisheng could make such a claim. Although unstated, it is unlikely that either family had a claim to northern roots. The fact that they are identified as natives of a frontier garrison town and that both served under the governor of another garrison town suggests quite strongly that whatever their family heritage they were not considered to be full members of the civilized community; as young men both were culturally suspect in the eyes of the court elite. Hu Fan, on the one hand, overcame the social hurdles that were in his way and had a notable career primarily serving the Liu Song dynasty; this is what merited his biography. Luo, on the other hand, was recognized for his extraordinary loyalty to the Jingzhou governor, a man of indecisive temperament who dilly-dallied in the face of a nativist rebellion. Although Luo had been advised by many, including Hu Fan, that the wishy-washy governor had no chance of defeating the rebels, he upheld his obligation to the man to the point of his death when indeed the rebels won.

Whether of elite or common heritage, the northern immigrants lived alongside if not actually among the indigenous population, who were most frequently known in northern sources either as *man* or *yue*, non-specific ethnonyms used to distinguish the southern other from the civilized. We have no way of estimating numbers, but logic suggests that deep into the Tang if not longer native southerners, whether of indigenous ethnicity or long-lost northern roots, outnumbered the northern immigrants; this, after all, was their land. Not surprisingly, relations between the two groups were not always smooth. Indeed, through the short life of the third-century Wu empire that ruled the South after the Han the Sinitic court regularly sought to control the "mountain Yue (*shanYue*)" as their records referred to the indigenous population. The Wu military regularly used "scorched Earth" tactics, a policy of intimidation that ultimately led to the "mountain Yue" submitting.

It should not be a surprise, therefore, that such tactics led to outbursts of rebellion such as that leading to the death of Luo Qisheng. The most striking case of southern resistance to Sinitic dominance, however, was the rebellion of Sun En (d. 402) across the turn of the fifth century against the Jin dynasty and the hegemonic power of the northern refugees that surrounded the court. The rebellion threw the Hangzhou Bay region into turmoil. Most tellingly, the upheaval saw the immigrant poor and alienated indigenes working together.

Sun En's own ethnicity is unclear. His standard biography identifies him with "the lineage of Sun Xiu," a prominent figure in the years following the southern relocation of the Jin dynasty.[7] Tradition links Sun Xiu to the imperial family of the third-century Wu dynasty that was also surnamed Sun. If we are to believe this, it would plausibly establish Sun Xiu and so his descendant Sun En as southerners with a northern heritage traced through the Wu imperial family. Because descent lines traced in ancient records are problematic and subject to a great deal of outright falsification, this claim must be considered suspect. It cannot, however, be entirely ignored, which leaves open the ironic possibility that Sun En, leader of the most significant rebellion against the Sinitic hegemony of the Jin court, was himself ethnically Sinitic.

With this background in mind, it is notable that when the Jin dynasty emerged from the ancient northern homeland to briefly reunify all of the Sinitic world late in the third century, Sun Xiu embarked on a complicated relationship with the new order that ended in his own rebellion and death. A century or so later, between 399 and his death in 402, Sun En led his followers on a destructively bloody rebellion arising from the off-shore islands along the coast in the Yangtze delta region and south as far as Hangzhou Bay. In the orthodox historical tradition this earned him the scornful title "sorcerer bandit (*yaozei*)," a belittlement used to define the rebels considered most threatening to the Sinitic order. In Sun En's case, when the court dispatched forces to confront him as he led his forces in campaigns on the mainland, he simply fled back to the islands that were his base and refuge. Lacking the capacity or desire to mount an off-shore campaign, the court forces would

---

[7] The following derives principally from Sun's biography in the *Jin shu*, j.100, and relevant passages in ZZTJ.

retreat to the security of the capital region, again and again allowing Sun En to reoccupy the nearby coastal mainland.

Beyond the routine accounts of pillage and assassination, the record of Sun's rebellion is frustratingly vague, yet there are multiple hints that he drew his support largely from the indigenous peoples. For example his forces are referred to as "wasps."[8] In English this may only suggest annoyance, but because the Chinese ideograph is based on the deeply insulting "bug" radical it gains a degree of dismissal that is not apparent otherwise.[9] Sun himself exhorted his forces by invoking Goujian, the semi-legendized ruler of the ancient "barbarian" Yue kingdom that had emerged on the shores of the Hangzhou Bay in the mid-first millennium BCE. As has been described in Chapter 1, Goujian had led his people in a successful challenge to the power of the Central Plain that briefly threatened the political order of the Plain, and even today he remains exemplary of barbarian danger.[10] He seems an unlikely model to have invoked, unless Sun was appealing to the historical memory of the men he led for whom Goujian might have evoked a sense of ethnic pride.

Further evidence that Sun relied on non-Sinitic support is his apparent reliance on the nautical skills of the indigenous peoples to build his naval fleet of "over one thousand 'tower boats.'"[11] On this the *Jin shu* comments, "The vessels were extraordinary. The 'hundred surnames' could not do this."[12] The "hundred surnames" has an ancient lineage as a term the elite used to refer to the common mass in orthodox culture; it is unlikely that it would be used to refer to non-Sinitic masses. Not only did the latter commonly lack

---

8 *Jin shu* 100:32b & ZZTJ 111:3499.
9 There are two features of Chinese characters that are relevant here. First is the radical. At least since compilation of the first dictionary of the Sinitic language in the first century CE, Chinese characters have been organized according to 214 radicals. The radical is a component part of all characters that points in a very general sense to the character's meaning. In Chinese dictionaries the radical functions much as western dictionaries arrange words by their initial letter. The second feature is the phoneme. Although not universal to all characters, when present the phoneme is a phonetic element that provides an equally general guide to pronunciation. In the case of "wasp" 蜂 (*feng*), the radical is 虫. All radicals can stand as their own character; as such 虫 means "bug." Characters with the "bug" radical have something to do with insects; when applied to ethnic groups the intent is deeply insulting. The right side of the character: 夆, although also a character in its own right, here is a phonetic guide to pronunciation; almost all characters with this component are pronounced "feng" in contemporary Mandarin.
10 See, for example, Cohen, *Speaking of History*.
11 ZZTJ 112:3524.
12 *Jin shu* 100:34b.

surnames, but the "hundred surnames" were the common folk of the Sinitic world, who did use surnames. The implication is that the people who built Sun's navy were not of the "hundred surnames." The conclusion reached by many, albeit without further evidence, is they must have been non-Sinitic adherents. As I explain below, however, one overlooked piece of evidence affirms this conclusion.

In 402, Sun En was killed and leadership of his revolt devolved upon his brother-in-law Lu Xun. Following Sun's death Lu led the surviving remnant of Sun's forces in flight down the coast to Guangzhou, which he seized. The complex ethnic makeup of the population of the deep South combined with its remote location may have made Guangzhou a safe redoubt. Lu, however, was not content. In 410 he launched an ill-conceived campaign into the Yangtze valley, which ended in disaster. He was killed and his rebellion was quelled.

Yet that is not the end. The final link between the rebellion and the "uncivilized" indigenous peoples of the South, and the link that leads us back to our story of Wu Xing and the Distributed Blessings Retention Dam, comes in its aftermath. In his discussion of Quanzhou (Fujian) in the *Universal Geography of the Taiping Era*, the geographical survey of the empire compiled on the heels of the Song restoration of the holistic empire in the late tenth century, the geographer Yue Shi tells us:

> The *quan lang* are the barbarian households of the prefecture. They are also known as the floating-boat people. They are the remnants [of the forces] of Lu Xun ... [Following Lu's defeat] the survivors escaped and scattered across the mountains and seas. Some endure to this day.[13]

Following Lu Xun's defeat, the survivors had scattered across the South, finding refuge among their non-Sinitic ethnic brethren in the mountainous interior and along the coastal fringe where Sinitic settlement as yet was often light if not nonexistent. As late as the last decades of the tenth century, when Yue Shi compiled his geography, their descendants had survived outside the bounds of the Sinitic world. They were regarded by those who adhered to orthodoxy as barbarian and bandits. Yue Shi refers to these survivors as the *quan lang*. He further identified them as the "barbarian households of [Quanzhou] prefecture ... the 'floating boat people.'" *Quan lang*, it appears, was a self-referential term; perhaps it was not even Sinitic, but a phonetic rendering of such a term. What is clear, and affirms the common interpretation, the survivors of Lu Xun's rebellion, themselves the survivors of the collapse of

---

13 *Taiping huanyuji* (Taipei: Wenhai chubanshe, 1962 reprint of 1803 ed.), 102:2b.

Sun En's rebellion, were not Sinitic; they were "barbarians," some of whom lived in the upland interior and others on the off-shore islands where the agriculturally oriented Sinitic immigrants let them be.

This was the world in which Wu Xing constructed the Distributed Blessings Retention Dam. As has been noted, we know very little about him. Although we cannot discount the possibility that Wu was a product of the indigenous culture of the central Fujian coast and Mulan River basin, the evidence reviewed in earlier chapters strongly suggests he was ethnically Sinitic. We can neither reliably conclude where his family might have come from nor how long his kin had been in the region. Regardless of his own origins, he was committed to the Sinitic economic model embraced in the classical four occupations: scholar, peasant, artisan and merchant. Among the most famous summations of this is by the fourth-century BCE Confucian scholar Mengzi, who wrote, "There are those who labor with their minds, and those who labor with their strength. Those who labor with their minds govern those who labor with their strength. Those who are ruled by others feed the people, and those who rule are fed by others" (Chapter 3A, section 4). Ban Gu (32–92 CE), author of the *Book of Han*, put it more fully:

> Scholars, peasants, artisans, and merchants are the Four People. Those who secure position through study are the scholars. Those who till the soil and raise crops are the peasants. Those who skillfully make goods are artisans. Those who trade in the exchange of goods are merchants.[14]

If Mengzi focused specifically and narrowly on the relationship between those who governed and the peasants who labored on the soil to provide food, Ban Gu extended his economic hierarchy to emphasize that those who "feed the people," though inferior to those who "labor with their minds," are more fundamental than those who make or trade in goods. In a world ruled by scholars, in other words, the foundation of the economy was agriculture. The most important product of agriculture, moreover, was grain. Throughout the imperial era before Wu Xing and his dam, among the principal media in which taxes had been collected was grain, be it wheat, sorghum, gaoliang or rice; although some taxes were paid in cloth, they were not collected in fruits, vegetables or animal products, all of which had to be converted into the grain equivalent for tax purposes.

The Distributed Blessings Retention Dam, which drained coastal marshland in order to make it suitable for agriculture, was entirely consistent with

---

14 *Han shu* 24a:2b.

this model. Wu Xing did not intend to improve the harvest of fish or game, on which the hunter–gatherers of the indigenous culture had long relied, nor is there any reason to believe that he was thinking of possible commercial connections with an outside world that might have recommended cultivation of crops such as fruits or fibers that were intended for the market, for such connections were as yet undeveloped. This was, as noted earlier, an agricultural project pure and simple, on which Commander Wu was prepared to expend considerable capital, both fiscal and political. But this was far more than an agricultural project. His conversion of what the Sinitic model regarded as the unproductive marshes of the Plain of Emerging Transformation into some of the Sinitic world's most bounteous agricultural lands was as much a rejection of the economy and culture of the pre-Sinitic inhabitants as it was a positive economic program. Wu Xing was displacing an indigenous economic pattern with an imported one, and in doing so he was displacing the indigenous people.

There is no way to know how many indigenous people may have lived around the periphery or on the tufts of dry land that dotted the marshland before Wu Xing's project. Census data survive, although the early numbers are unreliable. A census of the late third century, for example, abandoning any claim to accuracy, cited exactly 8,600 households across all Fujian, evenly divided between the coastal and interior prefectures. Another compilation from roughly two centuries later found precisely 2,843 households with 19,838 individuals scattered through the coastal prefectures.[15] While the latter data aspired to greater precision, neither census plausibly counts more than registered households that were either ethnically or culturally Sinitic, which could not have been more than a portion of the total population. By the mid-eighth century, only a few years before Wu undertook his project, the number of registered households had expanded markedly. Now there were slightly more than 30,000 households in greater Quanzhou, which at the time in addition to the metropolitan district on the Jin River covered both the Mulan River basin including Putian and its hinterland district Xianyou as well as the Jiulong River basin that became Zhangzhou.[16]

Numbers such as this suggest precision, but, as was discussed in the opening chapter, it is impossible to be certain what percentage of actual households were counted; it is easier, in fact, to guess which were not. Most simply, only

---

15 Chen Jingsheng, *Fujian lidai renkou lunkao* (Fuzhou: Fujian renmin, 1991), Table 2. All traditional Chinese population data were based on the number of households, a very fungible term that was rarely defined; counts of individuals are rare, and rules on which individuals might be counted varied over time and place.
16 Li Jifu, *Yuanhe junxian tuzhi* (Beijing: Zhonghua shuju, 1983), 29:719.

those that were officially registered were included. Unregistered households, no doubt including the overwhelming majority of the non-Sinitic indigenous households, have left no record. In areas where imperial authority was well-rooted and strong such as the Central Plain unregistered households might not have been a major factor. In peripheral areas such as the Fujian coast, on the other hand, when Wu Xing oversaw his project in the later eighth century, imperial authority remained weak and the ethnically and culturally non-Sinitic indigenous population was significant. Certainly much of the indigenous population—indeed, very possibly most of that population—was as yet unregistered. Conversely, because Sinitic households were most likely to be those registered on the official household registers that the Tang legal code required, it is equally correct to assume that the households counted in the early censuses of Fujian consisted heavily of Sinitic immigrants even though they may have been a minority of all who lived in the region.

The cultural tensions between northerners and southerners endured deep into the Tang dynasty. However, as has been noted in Chapter 1, historians know how events unfolded. We know that eventually these tensions were resolved. That is what our discussion turns to in the following chapter.

Chapter 5

THE SONG CONSOLIDATION AND SINITIC ACCOMMODATION

Our data on the local population between Wu Xing's project and the later tenth century are spotty. Soon after the mid-eighth century census that is referenced in Chapter 4 provided the first somewhat credible count of registered households in greater Quanzhou, however, the northern core of the empire was wracked by the rebellion associated with An Lushan. This prompted a major wave of migration toward the comparative safety of the South, which remained largely unaffected and relatively stable. It is reasonable, therefore, to assume that Wu Xing was prompted to undertake construction of the Distributed Blessings Retention Dam and drainage of the coastal salt marsh partially if not primarily in response to pressure for land that was a result of a growing presence of the agriculturally oriented Sinitic immigrants.

That presence is attested by the next trove of census data compiled in the latter half of the tenth century. By the turn of the tenth century, faced with a growing pattern of rebellion that culminated with an uprising in the 870s and 880s from which the dynasty was unable to recover, the Tang court had unraveled. In the power vacuum that followed a congeries of autonomous and mutually hostile regional warlords competed for power. When all had shaken out and the Tang court had been formally deposed early in the tenth century, the Tang realm was a divided world. From a base on the Central Plain, the old heartland of Sinitic power and cultural authority, one leader claimed to have inherited the mantle of the Tang mandate and proclaimed a new dynasty called Liang. Along the length of the Yangtze River basin and across the deeper South, however, the struggle to fill the vacuum led to seven autonomous courts, each claiming their own share of the imperial mandate. The narrative of the interregnum decades that followed is complex and largely not relevant to our discussion.[1] After several decades of division, however, a new order began to emerge from the Central Plain. This was the Song dynasty.

---

1 For detailed treatment of this era, see Hugh R. Clark, "The Southern Kingdoms Between the T'ang and Sung," in *The Cambridge History of China*, vol. 5, Part One, "The Sung Dynasty and its Precursors, 907–1279," edited by Denis Twitchett and Paul Jakov

The Song court, which claimed the imperial mandate in 960, inherited from the Latter Zhou, the last of the interregnum northern dynasties, a policy of imperial reintegration. The new dynasty tackled the autonomous courts of the South one by one. As each court surrendered to the Song mandate, some voluntarily and others in the face or reality of force, updated population data were collected, all of which reflected significant growth in the number of registered households. Of most relevance to this discussion is the data from Fujian, which with the collapse of the Tang had fallen under the rule of a chronically unstable court based in the Min River basin of northern Fujian that called itself Min. When that court collapsed in an orgy of assassination in the 940s, the coastal river basins of central and southern Fujian: the Mulan, Jin and Jiulong, fell under the rule of an autonomous warlord; this was the Quan/Zhang warlord satrapy. When the last of the Quan/Zhang warlords submitted to the Song in 978, he presented a new census that in addition to surging numbers in the Jin and Jiulong basins counted almost 34,000 households in Xinghua Prefecture, a new administrative unit covering only the Mulan River basin that included Putian and its hinterland district Xianyou. This was the first time the basin had independent demographic data (see Table 5.1).[2]

No doubt these numbers in part reflected a more thorough count of the population that was already resident, including for example those who had dispersed through the interior and avoided earlier censuses. The data may also represent the first systematic effort to count non-Sinitic households. Nevertheless, there is ample, albeit again largely anecdotal, evidence that the turmoil that wracked the North throughout the interregnum century prompted renewed waves of migration toward the South. Many were now

Table 5.1 Registered population of Xinghua Commandery, tenth to thirteenth centuries.

Date	Number of Households	Source
978	33,735	TPHYJ 102:10b
1080	55,237	YFJYZ 9:14b
ca. 1190	72,363	PYBS 1:3b-4a

Note: TPHYJ, *Taiping huanyuji* (Taipei: Wenhai chubanshe, 1962 reprint of 1803 ed.); YFJYZ, *Yuanfeng jiuyu zhi* (ESKQS ed.) and PYBS, *Puyang bishi* (Wanwei biezang ed.)

Smith (Cambridge: Cambridge University Press, 2009), 133–205. See also Hugh R. Clark, *China During the Tang-Song Interregnum, 878–978* (London: Routledge, 2022).

2 In fact, the new prefecture was not established until two years later, in 980. Thus, the separate data reflect either a delayed compilation of the census or an adjustment of figures by the Song. For our purposes, the distinction is moot.

finding their way into the, as yet comparatively, lightly settled coastal plains of Fujian. Nor, as the following censuses indicate, did the growth in registered population stop in the decades and centuries that followed. By the later twelfth century, in fact, the registered population had more than doubled.

It will never be possible to know the exact balance of family background within those ca. 34,000 households counted in 978. Most were illiterate peasants who survive for us only in abstract numbers; they will forever remain entirely anonymous. Only the elite who left us some kind of record of their existence allow us to go beyond the numbers. We can divide this elite into three groups: (1) early immigrants, families that had established themselves well before the collapse of the Tang dynasty in the late ninth century; (2) indigenous families who had successfully adapted to the new dominance of the Sinitic world; and (3) immigrants who had been driven south by turmoil in the imperial heartland accompanying the Tang collapse.

Many families that flourished in later centuries had traditions that placed them among the first group. Wu Xing could be exemplary, but as noted we know almost nothing about him and so we have no way of verifying his origins; there is, moreover, no solid evidence that he was able to extend his prominence and wealth to later heirs.[3] Much more, however, can be said about others, such as the Zheng clan of Putian. Their tradition claimed that the founding ancestor had fled the North in the face of the early fourth-century upheavals that forced the Jin court to flee to the Yangtze basin. He is alleged to have found refuge in northern Fujian, as is explained in the earliest preface to a family genealogy: "Our ancestors initially settled in Houguan district in Fuzhou [i.e., the Min River basin in northern Fujian]."[4] The preface then continues:

> As gentry households fled south to escape troubles [the three brothers] Lu, Zhuang, and Shu left Houguan ... and proceeded together to South Lake Mountain in Putian where they settled by the graves of their ancestors.

---

3 There was a prominent Wu lineage in Putian that produced a significant number of examination graduates through the Song; see Clark, *Portrait of a Community; Society, Culture, and the Structures of kinship in the Mulan River Valley (Fujian) from the Late Tang through the Song* (Hong Kong: Chinese University Press, 2007), especially Appendix 2. Although modern Wu genealogical records claim descent from the Song lineage and that Wu Xing had been their founding ancestor, there is no record from the Song that makes this claim.

4 Zheng Donglao, 1169 genealogical preface, quoting an undated genealogical preface by Zheng Qiao (1104–62), in *Nanhu Zhengshi dazongpu* (collection of the Library of Fuzhou Shifan University), no pagination. A much later preface claimed the three brothers had migrated to Putian in 743.

Although Zheng records claim this was in the sixth century, other sources conclusively place the three brothers in the mid-eighth century; that is when the move by the brothers to Putian occurred.[5] At some point, the descendants of the purported founding ancestor in Houguan district had established a family burial ground in the vicinity of South Lake Mountain on the edge of the interior highlands that lie immediately behind the Putian prefectural city. The graves lay adjacent to a Buddhist monastery that had been established in the sixth century. In order to care for the graves, some in the family apparently settled in the area; the three brothers had joined these relatives.

The Zheng and their history are exemplary of early Sinitic settlers, many of whom have left similarly confusing accounts as *de classé* refugees constructed narratives that bestowed luster on long venerated ancestors. The Huang who lived on the northern coast of Putian offer a different picture that illustrates the second group. Like the Zheng, the Huang claim to have descended from a fourth-century migrant who had arrived in the Min River basin in the face of the northern invasions. Family records, however, have nothing more to say about that. Instead, they turn to one Huang An. Having served as a regional official in western Guangnan (modern Guangxi) in the 750s, family tradition says that he was returning to the family home in the Min River basin when he was enraptured by the beautiful Putian coastline and chose to relocate.[6]

There are two reasons to wonder about the Huangs' claimed northern roots. First, unlike the records of the Zheng, which provide a partial record of the family experience between their arrival in the Min basin and when the three brothers removed to Putian, the Huang records say nothing of their experience between their reputed arrival in the fourth century and Huang An's relocation in the mid-eighth century—the same time, it bears noting, that the three Zheng brothers also relocated to Putian. Second, Huang An's service among the non-Sinitic peoples of western Guangnan is the kind of appointment commonly filled by men who had passed through a special recruitment system called "southern selection." This was a facilitated examination process that was implemented as a way to recruit men of the South to hold low-level local offices across the South. Men recruited this way were not part of the standing bureaucracy, but whether they were ethnically indigenous or had a long legacy of living among the non-Sinitic indigenes, as southerners they were presumably familiar both with the ways of their southern peers

---

5 See my discussions in *Portrait of a Community*, 38–39, 264–68 and elsewhere.
6 Huang Yanhui (1124 *jinshi*), untitled/undated dedicatory preface to *Puyang Qiongxi Huangshi zongpu* (undated Qing dynasty edition, collection of the library of Fuzhou Shifan University), no pagination.

and accustomed to the rigors of the southern climate. This leaves us at least some reason to think the Huang may have tried to cover up an indigenous background with bogus claims to northern roots.

The Fang of the Putian district town, who went on to become one of the most illustrious extended families of the Song, are exemplary of the third group, immigrants who had arrived in the context of the Tang collapse. The ancestors of the first Fang in Putian had lived for an unknown length of time across two prefectures in the mountainous interior of modern Zhejiang province that lies just north of Fujian. They were, in other words, southerners, although whether they were descendants of migrants from the Sinitic North or truly indigenous is unknowable as the family's history remains undocumented until the last decades of the Tang. That their history begins at the point when the first Fang received an imperial appointment suggests that before then they may have held the minor offices in local government through "southern selection."

Facing a nearly complete loss of legitimacy when confronted with widespread rebellion in the last years of the ninth century, the Tang court desperately sought to sustain support among regional elites by recruiting officials such as the Fang into the regular bureaucracy from which the "southern selection" officers heretofore had been excluded. Family records assert that the grandfather of Fang Tingfan, the first to settle in Putian and with whom family history begins, had served in the retinue of an unidentified military governor. Very likely this had been one of the numerous local warlords across the South whose *de facto* power had been given official status by the court even before the cataclysmic rebellion that marked the effective end of Tang authority erupted in the 870s. Like many who were disillusioned with the Tang but even more fearful of the chaos they saw spreading from the rebellion, Tingfan's father had fought on behalf of the beleaguered court. In 884, as rebel leadership was killed and their rebellion collapsed, the Tang court attempted to reconsolidate its authority. This gentleman was rewarded with a staff position in the imperial Censorate. In further recognition of his contributions, his son Tingfan was given a succession of district magistracies in Fujian. As the last remnants of Tang authority crumbled in the last decade of the ninth century and the Central Plain was thrown into unresolved chaos, Tingfan decided to settle in the Putian district city, his last post, allegedly because the stability of the area appealed to him.[7]

Like others who fit their profile, as the Tang collapsed and political authority devolved toward more local levels, Tingfan's family quickly assumed a

---

7 On this and following, see Fang Dacong, "Fangshi zupu xi," *Tieanji*, roll 32.

leading role in local society. His six sons all held office in autonomous Fujian during the decades of the Tang–Song interregnum. Following the Song reconsolidation, his later descendants were among the empire's leading families on the lists of examination graduates. Many were prominent in the Song bureaucracy and their marriage connections encompassed a broad range of the empire's elite.[8]

All these traditions might seem to affirm the narrative that exalts the triumph of Sinitic culture and identity across the barbaric lands of the South. But it was not that simple. Consider the deity known formally today as the Empress of Heaven (*Tianhou*), an imperial title that was bestowed on her with the emperor's blessing in the eighteenth century. Among her myriad devotees, she is most often known as the "Maternal Ancestor" (*Mazu*). Before any of that, however, before anyone outside the central coastal regions of Fujian knew anything about her, she was simply the Divine Woman of Meizhou, named for a small island that lies between the Mulan River basin and Quanzhou where her cult was first celebrated. By whichever name, she has long been one of the most important deities in the Chinese pantheon. But that is a story of the interaction between the encroaching Sinitic world and the world of local culture along the central Fujian coast, the area where Wu Xing constructed his Distributed Blessings Retention Dam.[9]

In 1150 Liao Pengfei, a native of the Putian region who is otherwise virtually unknown, wrote an inscription that commemorated the restoration and renaming of a shrine located on a mound near the mouth of the Mulan River in Putian that was dedicated to the Divine Woman.[10] The mound rose above the surrounding marshes that had largely remained undrained until the eleventh century—in other words, this was precisely the kind of marginal location that remained unsuitable for agriculture and so sheltered from the Sinitic incursion. Liao explained that late in the eleventh century the cult of the Divine Woman had migrated from its place of origin in Meizhou. The restoration of the shrine that Liao celebrated was undertaken in prepara-

---

8 See Clark, *Portrait of a Community*, passim.
9 Among the many contemporary works that discuss the Divine Woman, see Hansen, *Changing Gods in Medieval China, 1127–1276*, and James L. Watson, "Standardizing the Gods: The Promotion of T'ien-hou ('Empress of Heaven') Along the South China Coast, 960–1960," in *Popular Culture in Late Imperial China*, edited by David Johnson, Andrew J. Nathan, and Evelyn S. Rawski (Berkeley: University of California Press, 1985), 292–324. On the question of what constitutes a Chinese deity, see Clark, "What Makes a Chinese God? or What Makes a God Chinese?," 111–139.
10 Liao Pengfei, "Shengdun zumiao chongjian Shunji miao ji," in the *Baitang Lishi zupu* (privately held, no pagination). The text is reproduced in Dean & Zheng, *Xinghua*, 15–17.

tion for receipt of an imperial plaque of recognition, a step that granted the shrine and the Divine Woman imperial recognition and protected them from the possibility that they could be denounced by officials as heterodox. Liao explained that the Divine Woman was the deified spirit of a female shaman. In life, she "could foretell a man's luck or misfortune. When she died the people erected a shrine on her home island." Although later tradition claimed that the Divine Woman had lived in the latter half of the tenth century, Liao, who was the first to write about her, admitted that no one knew the origins of her cult.

In the absence of any further information, there is obviously a risk in suggesting more, but for several reasons it seems that the Divine Woman in fact had emerged within the indigenous, pre-Sinitic culture of the southeast coast. At least there can be little doubt that her cult had emerged on the islands that dot the Putian coast. We know almost nothing about the early history of these islands, but we should recall the *quan lang* who have been introduced in the preceding chapter. They were "the barbarian households of Quanzhou prefecture," refugees who had "scattered across the mountains and seas" following the final collapse of Sun En's rebellion at the beginning of the fourth century. The *quan lang* were exemplary of the indigenous, non-Sinitic people who had long found refuge on the off-shore islands, the islands where the cult of the Divine Woman had emerged, even as Sinitic settlers had solidified their control of the adjacent mainland. The Divine Woman, in other words, was almost certainly the product of a non-Sinitic local culture with deep historical roots.

In the decades and centuries that followed, however, she became an integral part of the Sinitic world. The key was her presumed role in saving the imperial envoy Lu Yundi, who had been dispatched in 1123 on a diplomatic mission to the Korean Koguryo kingdom. On his return voyage across the Yellow Sea, his fleet was caught in a dreadful storm. The details of what happened vary depending on whose account one reads. Some say that seven of eight vessels in Lu's entourage sank; others claim all eight vessels safely reached the empire's shores. What all agree on, however, is that at the height of the storm a deity appeared at the top of the mast of at least one ship and danced. That ship, perhaps only that ship, survived. Who—or what—danced atop the mast was a matter of debate. We can guess that what the men aboard this ship saw was St. Elmo's Fire, a rare but real meteorological event that appears in intense electrical storm as fire at the top of pointed structures such as masts and church steeples. Those who survived the disaster in the middle of the Yellow Sea, however, had no doubt that it was a deity offering plrotection, but not all saw the same deity. At least one man, however, knew it was the Divine Woman. This was Li Zhen, who petitioned the throne to recognize the deity's role in protecting its envoy.

We do not know very much concretely about Li Zhen, except that he was a native of Putian and a kinsman to Li Fu, a man of substantial wealth which he used for the general benefit of his kin and neighbors. He underwrote, for example, the construction and restoration of Buddhist temples, he financed reconstruction of the Putian prefectural school, he constructed sea walls "to protect the people's livelihood," and he built bridges and shelters "to give comfort to travelers"–and all was "financed from his own resources." Above all he acquired a large library, which he made available to his kin as they prepped for the imperial exams.[11] Li Fu also financed the 1150 renovations to the Shrine of the Holy Mound done in preparation for receiving the imperial placard. Liao tells us that Li Fu "donated 70,000 of his own cash" toward the restoration, a dramatic demonstration of Li Fu's commitment to the cult of the Divine Woman. Liao Pengfei, was Li Fu's secretary. He recounts that he composed the inscription at Li Fu's request.

Although the Divine Woman, soon to be widely known as the Maternal Ancestor (*Mazu*), was a local deity patronized by the non-Sinitic coastal culture, by the early twelfth century the boundary between that culture and Sinitic culture, the boundary between the much wider range of non-Sinitic cultures and the Sinitic culture all were encountering, was eroding. The Divine Woman did not become Sinitic; that was not her world. But as the savior of the imperial envoy, she did transcend the limits of her natal culture. Liao Pengfei had been drafted by his mentor, a powerful and wealthy local figure, to compose the inscription for her shrine atop the mound that commemorated receipt of the imperial plaque.

Both the inscription and the plaque were archetypically Sinitic. The inscription was a record (*ji*), a literary genre that was fully embraced by the orthodox academic culture; shrines that were commemorated with a record were almost by definition embraced by that orthodox world. The imperial plaque that was bestowed on her shrine granted her cult formal recognition; she was no longer the cult deity of a marginal community that sat aside but not as a part of the Sinitic world. She was now a deity that had received

---

11 Attested in Huang Gongdu, "Song dianqian zhigan Danxuan Li xiansheng Meifeng shuyuan bei," in Dean & Zheng, *Xinghua*, 17–18. See also Xu Shiren, "Meizi gangwo yun xuan ji," in Ibid., 19–20. The Qing dynasty Fujian provincial gazetteer links twenty-nine bridges to Li Fu; see Chen Shouqi, et al., *(Tongzhi) Fujian tongzhi* (Taibei: Huawen shuju, 1968 reprint of 1871 edition), 29:24a–26a.

imperial sanction. She was now a Chinese deity, and the culture that venerated her was consolidating as Chinese culture, a culture that traces its roots to the ancient Sinitic culture of the Central Plain but that has adapted to the myriad non-Sinitic cultures it has encountered.

We are thus left with a complex world. Like the cult of the Divine Woman, families such as the Zheng, the Huang and the Fang, whatever the realities of their backgrounds, were committed to the values of orthodox Sinitic culture. In the decades after the Song reconsolidation of empire, each was a regular participant in the imperial examinations that exalted those values and only those values. Among the elite, the public embrace of Sinitic culture was an essential feature. But the pre-Sinitic indigenous culture of the *quan lang* survived in the marginal spaces such as the off-shore islands. The relationship between the orthodox Sinitic world and the ecstatic world of the indigenous culture had long been problematic, but the Divine Woman became a bridge between the two.

Chapter 6

THE ECOLOGICAL AND ENVIRONMENTAL CONSEQUENCES

To this point, our discussion has focused on social and cultural changes, but what of changes to the land? In the deep historical past, before China's landscape was radically altered by the hand of man, the North presented the flat but forested horizons of the Central Plain. Beyond the Taihang Mountains that mark the western edge of the Plain lay the broken landscape of the river basins that cut the friable soils called loess. Rainfall across the North is irregular, although in ancient times evidence suggests it was more plentiful than today. Nevertheless, although the soils are fertile and easy to till, the rivers and other water sources could dry up, as they do today. Without irrigation, agriculture is unreliable for crops are likely to wither and die.[1]

In contrast, the South was a land of mountains and forests, riven by valleys marked by free-flowing rivers. Rainfall is abundant, the rivers are broad and the landscape is dotted with lakes, large and small. There was a wide and abundant diversity of plant and animal life: snakes and fish, deer, birds and mammals big and small, even tigers, rhinoceros and elephants. Liu Zongyuan wrote from his exile in the deepest South that the world around him was filled with unfamiliar noises and scents. It was a world that Liu and his colleagues feared.[2] To many, however, the South was both exotic and seductive, so much so that phlegmatic northerners worried that it could captivate and corrupt the unwary, turn them away from the stern moral values on which northern culture was based, and convert them into hedonistic barbarians. As the late eighth-century poet Bao He wrote to a friend about going South as an official:

---

[1] For this and the discussion that follows, see Robert B. Marks, *China: An Environmental History*, 2nd ed. (Lanham, MD: Rowman & Littlefield, 2017), 22–26, and Mark Elvin, *The Retreat of the Elephants: An Environmental History of China* (New Haven: Yale University Press, 2004), especially 19–85. A more recent treatment that considers a narrower range of issues is Felt, *Structures of the Earth*.

[2] Schafer, *Vermilion Bird*, is the best discussion in English of the fear of the South among northern literati.

> Grasping jade, the barbarians come to our land from afar,
> Bearing pearls they time and again bring tribute.
> For many years you will see no snow.
> Wherever you go it will be spring.[3]

For those willing to bear its challenges, this was a land filled with opportunity. The verdant bottomlands and coastal plains had rich soils that beckoned to be tilled. Its exotic products: fruits such as oranges, bananas, lychee and longyan, medicinals such as rhino horn and elephant tusk, and exotic meats and herbs, found ready markets in the cities of the North. But it was also filled with dangers, both real and imaginary. Some were small and easy to overlook, as Liu Zongyuan lamented in a letter from his exile: "as I go about I find much to fear for through the wilds there are poisonous snakes and great wasps."[4] Others, however, were large and intrusive. Writing early in the Song dynasty, for example, Peng Cheng (1012 *jinshi*) noted that tigers abounded in the mountains of western Fujian; as late as 1266, in an inscription commemorating the restoration of a shrine in Quanzhou, the author praised the deity for protecting against the predations of tigers.[5] Peng Cheng also observed that elephants roamed about Zhangzhou, in southernmost Fujian, in herds of ten or more: "They are not dangerous to humans when in herds. It is only the solitary elephant that is dangerous,"[6] advice that remains as true today as it was then. The official *History of the Song Dynasty* noted that "rhinoceros and elephants" were among the goods the king of the autonomous kingdom of WuYue, located around the Hangzhou Bay, sent to the brand new Song court in 960—presumably meaning horn and ivory rather than the beasts themselves.[7] In 963 officials in Hubei in central China, in the first of a slew of similar events, reported that elephants were hiding in the forests, from where they would forage to eat the peoples' crops.[8] As late as 1171 a "wild herd of several hundred" elephants devoured the harvest in Chaozhou, which abuts Zhangzhou to the South.[9] Then there were rhinoceros. Collections such as

---

3 Bao He, "Song Li shijun fu Quanzhou" *(Yuding) QuanTang shi* 208:1a.
4 "Yu Lin Hanlin Jian shu" 與李翰林建書 *Liu hedong ji* 30:494–496, quoting from 494.
5 Wang Mengshou, "Haoshan miao peiji," in Kenneth Dean and Zheng Zhenman, editors, *Epigraphical Materials on the History of Religion in Fujian: Quanzhou Prefecture* (Fuzhou: Fujian Peoples Publishing House, 2003), vol. 3, 957–58.
6 Tao Zongyi, *Shuofu* (ESKQS ed.), 15b:41a & 42a. For a broader discussion of elephants, see Elvin, *The Retreat of the Elephants*.
7 *Song shi* (ESKQS ed.), 1:19a.
8 *Song shi* (ESKQS ed.), 66:18a.
9 *Song shi* (ESKQS ed.), 66:20a.

The Environs of Fiction, assembled by Tao Zongyi (b.1316) in the mid-fourteenth century, contain numerous references to belts of rhino skin and to medicines made of rhino horn, although few allude to the rhinoceros itself. It was the aforementioned Peng Cheng, however, who observed early in the eleventh century that the language of the *man* barbarians in the Southwest had a specific term for the rhino, strongly suggesting a familiarity.[10]

Among the threats, however, crocodiles were prominent. We have already discussed the beast legend calls a *jiao* that undercut the dikes of Wu Xing's Distributed Blessings drainage project (see Chapter 2). In the same chapter we have referenced that at almost the same time, so coincidental that one might wonder if it could have been linked to the same event, Han Yu wrote of what he also called a *jiao*, without a doubt a crocodile, that was threatening both people and livestock in southern Fujian: "If people approached [the lake] by mistake, or if a horse or cow came for a drink, they usually were eaten." This particular beast was killed when "a terrible commotion from within the mountain"—an earthquake?—led to a massive landslide that filled the lake with debris and crushed it.[11]

Han's encounter with crocodiles, moreover, was not limited to Fujian. We have referenced his encounter when enroute to his exile to Chaozhou. A minor official warned him, "The crocodiles are larger than boats, their teeth and eyes cause terror and death." While in Chaozhou, moreover he wrote his "Offering to the Crocodile," in which he ordered all the beasts to leave Chaozhou after receiving his sacrifice:

> You bug-eyed crocodiles do not bring peace to the streams and ponds. You eat the people and their cattle, bears, hogs, deer, and roebuck, all to fatten your bodies and nourish your young. [12]

Nor was Han Yu alone in lamenting the threat posed by crocodiles. For example, while in exile in the far southwest, his colleague Liu Zongyuan, with whom Han is closely linked, recounted several encounters with crocodiles, which he consistently called *jiao*, or sometimes *chi*, a cognate term with the same meaning. Most notably he tells of one such beast that terrorized the local people: "It had destroyed the river bank right up to the Southern city

---

10 Tao, *Shuo fu*, 15b:35b. Elvin, *The Retreat of the Elephants*, cites several references of rhinoceros, especially in "archaic times" when rhinoceros skin was used as armor; see 31–32.
11 Zhang Du, *Xuanshi zhi* (ESKQS ed.), 5:12b–13b and *Taiping guangji* (ESKQS ed.), 392:1a–1b.
12 For references, see Chapter 2.

gate. It overturned boats and killed the people, and then went away."[13] These comments were echoed by Han Ruoxun, a largely anonymous and undated Tang scholar and author: "The rivers of the deep south have crocodiles. They eat people and livestock."[14] Even as Sinitic settlement intensified crocodiles remained a problem along the southern coast. Ouyang Xiu, among the greatest figures of the eleventh century when the Sinitic imprint on the South was gaining momentum, noted that crocodiles continued to threaten peoples' lives in Chaozhou,[15] and Chen Li (1252–1335), writing more than two centuries later, lamented that he had heard that crocodiles in Guangzhou could chase down cattle and horses on land and kill them.[16]

Crocodiles, elephants and tigers, as well as noxious insects such as wasps, are all tangible. Those who wrote of them, and especially those who were plagued by them, knew all too well their reality. But there was also a sharp disease gradient between the dryland North and the humid South that was even more threatening because it was so much less understood. Parasitic diseases such as malaria, cholera and *schistosomiasis*, for example, were a constant threat, as were a range of viral and fungal illnesses; many were symptomatically recognized, but few were understood. This made it ideal as a place of exile for those the emperor wanted permanently out of the way. Wherever one turned, there was a wealth of creatures large and small, visible and otherwise, that threatened the unfamiliar with grievous harm, if not death.

This was the world Wu Xing knew before he launched his project; it was the world he set about to change. To fully grasp what his project accomplished, we must start again with what had been before. For untold eons, before the Putian district was established in the earliest years of the Tang dynasty, several free-flowing rivers had coursed through the mountainous upland terrain before they disgorged into a large, shallow coastal marsh (see Map 6.1). No descriptions of the marshland survive, but we can look to contemporary examples of such marsh to envision what it was like. Tidal waterways, a brackish mixture of salt and fresh, must have wound their way about tufts of marsh reeds. Here and there higher land poked out, land that lay high enough to stay dry as tides rose and fell, marked perhaps by the occasional tree. These are among the richest food sources on the planet—they support varieties of fish, mollusks, amphibians, birds and a wide range of vegetation that can be consumed or used to make things. We know that the indigenous people had lived on and around this

---

13 *Liu hedong ji* 10:7a.
14 Tao Zongyi, *Shuofu* (ESKQS ed.), 112b:17b.
15 *Ouyang wenzhong ji* (ESKQS ed.), 20:6a.
16 Tao, *Shuofu*, 109b:29a. In fact, over short distances crocodilians can outrun horses.

THE ECOLOGICAL AND ENVIRONMENTAL CONSEQUENCES   69

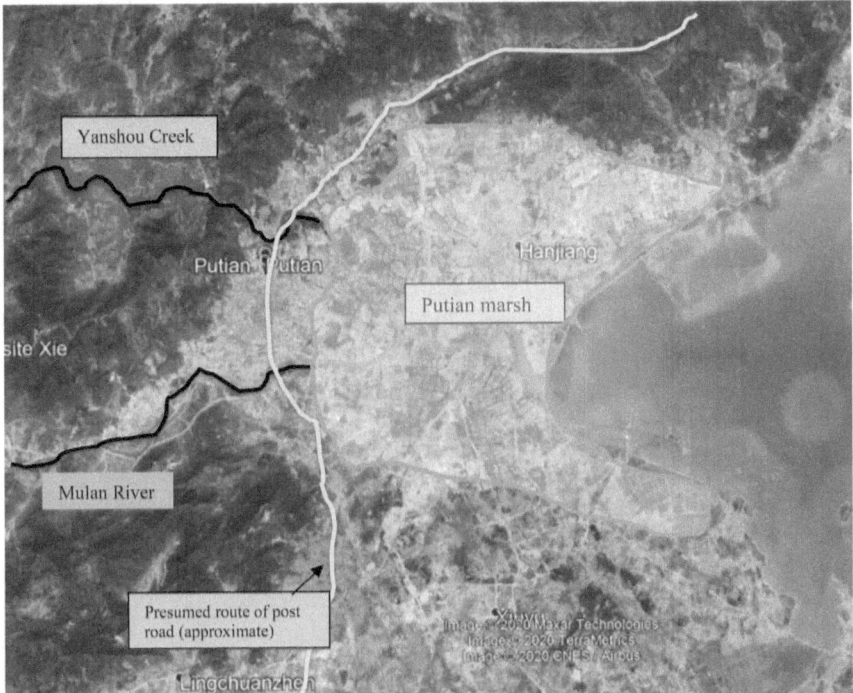

Map 6.1 A rough estimate of the original Putian coastline and Putian marsh. Source: Google Earth.

marsh for untold generations. Most material evidence of their presence on the marsh has long since been wiped out, but the Neolithic settlements found in the surrounding hills and the associated shell mounds discussed in earlier chapters survive. Remember as well that the *quan lang*, the "barbarian households" of Quanzhou, were also known as the "floating-boat people." The *quan lang* spent much of their lives on boats from which they exploited the riches of the seas and marshes. There is, moreover, one record that hints at the relationship between the indigenous people and the marsh.

When the cult of the Divine Woman of Meizhou spread to the Mulan River basin she initially joined two male deities that had long been enshrined on a hillock near the river's mouth. The only thing we know about these deities is negative. Liao Pengfei, author of the 1150 inscription introduced in Chapter 4 that is the only evidence of their cult at all, tells us, "I know nothing of their origins." We do not know how they were understood by their devotees. We do not know what services they were thought to provide. It is not possible today even to determine the exact location of their shrine, except that by the late eleventh century it lay down river from the prefectural city near what was then the mouth of the Mulan River. But there is one thing we can be quite certain about. Before the ongoing process of drainage and reclamation begun by Wu Xing late in the eighth century and carried on through the decades and centuries that followed had extended to the tuft where their cult was centered, the cult's shrine had been on an isolated hillock of dry land. We cannot know whether the hillock was surrounded by marsh or shallow open water, but it assuredly was one or the other, and their shrine sat on top of that rise. Perhaps for the untold eons before Wu Xing began the process of draining the marsh this had been a place where the *quan lang* could camp while they collected the marsh's bounty. Or perhaps they saw the hillock as a numinous site best left to the inchoate powers that could protect, or threaten, them.

Regardless, Liao continues that one night in 1086,

> a radiant light manifested itself on the hillock. The villagers could not explain it. A fisherman went out to investigate and found a raft.[17] He brought this to his house, but by the next day it had returned to its former place. That evening the people living near the hillock all had the same dream: "I am the Divine Woman of Meizhou. The raft in fact is the evidence [of my presence]. You should build me a retreat on the hillock." The elders thought this extraordinary, so they built a shrine, which they called the "Shrine of the Holy Hillock."

Apparently, a village of fishermen had taken shape at the base of the hillock. The raft that had washed ashore provides us a strong clue about these villagers. As described previously, to work the nearer coastal and marsh waters the indigenous people of the southeast coast had long used bamboo rafts, which are simple to build and remarkably stable (see Ill. 6.1). Because they have a very shallow draft, they are ideal for poking about the estuaries of just such a coastal marsh as must have once surrounded the hillock. The fisherman who found it knew right away how useful it could be and took it home.

Absent anything definitive, we can only guess that the fisherman and his peers identified themselves as *quan lang*. Regardless, their ancestors must have lived off the products of the marsh and the nearby open waters of Xinghua Bay. Wu Xing's Distributed Blessings reclamation project radically altered this relationship. In draining the marsh, even if he initially tackled only a small portion of it, he was redefining the relationship between the marsh and those who exploited it. As explained in Chapter 2, the Sinitic economy

---

17 The term I translate as "raft" (*cha*) could mean many things, including "sticks." I render it "raft" because the fisherman apparently recognized its utility, something sticks would not have had.

THE ECOLOGICAL AND ENVIRONMENTAL CONSEQUENCES 71

Ill. 6.1 A sample image of traditional construction of simple bamboo raft. Source: www.shutterstock.com/image-photo/old-bamboo-raft-floating-on-lake-257329558.

was primarily an agricultural economy, a point that is emphasized in the prefaces to the *Record of Water Conservancy in Putian*. This work, a collection of documents from the Tang through the nineteenth century, was assembled in 1875 to commemorate the several drainage projects, beginning with Wu Xing's Distributed Blessings, that had so altered the ecology of the Plain of Emerging Transformation and so changed the relationship between the plain and those who lived there. In a dedicatory preface a local official observed:

> Putian is surrounded by the sea on three sides. Since the Song a myriad of fields have been defended from salt marsh. All have become richly fertile behind the dikes that hold the freshwater. The virtue [of this project] is vast.[18]

A supplementary preface made a similar point from a different perspective:

> The natural world (*tian di*) bestows its own natural benefits, but if one does not know how to use them [i.e., if one leaves land unimproved] the benefits are not realized. Even if one does know how, if one cannot get people to come and if one cannot apply the principles of correct allocation, then one still will not realize the benefits.[19]

---

18 Chen Maolie, 1875 preface, *Putian shuili zhi* (Taipei: Chengwen, 1974 reprint of 1875 ed.), 1a.
19 Zhang Mengyuan, 1875 preface, *Putian shuili zhi*, 5a.

In the eyes of these commentators writing more than a millennium later, Wu Xing's project was the first step in transforming the marsh from what was considered useless into what was considered useful, into something that could be allocated to maximize its benefits. In short order, the now accessible land was occupied by new settlers who converted what had been wasteland into agriculturally productive fields and paddy. Nor did the transformation of the salt marsh that lay north of the Mulan River, what later commentators called the "northern farmland," stop with the work of Wu Xing. During the decades of the Min kingdom (909–45) that controlled Fujian for much of the Tang–Song Interregnum, three retention ponds were dug, extending irrigation beyond the eastern limits of the Distributed Blessings network along the foot of the upland fringe.[20] In the 960s, the Southern Peace Retention Dam further corralled the waters of the eastern upland fringe, pushing the drained land almost to its present extent. In the mid-eleventh century, pushed by a relentlessly expanding population, the waters that fed the three retention ponds were corralled by the Great Peace Retention Dam, providing irrigation to an additional 1,000 acres; the ponds themselves were converted to fields. And always peasants were pushing the coastal perimeter further and further into the Xinghua Bay, a process that continues even today.

By far the most famous project was the Mulan River Retention Dam (see Ill. 6.2) that diverted water from the Mulan River, which drained most of the prefectural interior, to the lands south of the river, what came to be known as the "southern farmland."[21] The Mulan is significantly larger than Distributed Blessings Creek. Consequently, damming it was a much more challenging project. At least since the Tang there had been efforts to convert the Southern marshes into viable cropland. The earliest efforts had been based around a series of retention ponds and had had only limited success. The success of Wu Xing's project and the development of the "northern farmland," however, had set a precedent; just as the fresh water of the Distributed Blessings Creek had made that reclamation possible, so it was determined a similar diversion of the Mulan would open vast new land for cultivation of the "southern farmland."

The first attempt to divert the waters of the Mulan River as Wu Xing had diverted those of the Distributed Blessings Creek was organized by Miss

---

20 This and all the following draws on the *Putian shuili zhi*, chapter three, which in turn relies primarily on Ming dynasty sources.
21 The term I am translating as "farmland" is *yang*, which most commonly means "ocean." An editorial comment in the *Putian shuili zhi* 2:5a, however, explains that in this context it means "level farmland" (*ping chou*).

Ill. 6.2 The Mulan River Retention Dam. Photo by author.

Chen in 1064. Her role in the endeavor is an intriguing mystery. She was a native of the Min River basin in northern Fujian; why she is connected to the project is unclear. A likely explanation, however, is that Miss Chen had married into a Putian family; such marriage links between Putian and the Fuzhou region of northern Fujian were not uncommon, and several families had links that endured across multiple generations.[22] She spent a large amount of her wealth to underwrite this attempt, and a dam was completed. Shortly after, however, it collapsed. Miss Chen in turn collapsed into a deep depression and threw herself into the river. A Ming dynasty commentator dismissively noted, "she was only a woman"![23] Soon after Lin Congshi, also from northern Fujian, made a second attempt; it too failed, leading the same commentator to note that "he was only an examination graduate."[24]

---

22 See *Portrait of a Community*, especially Chapter 4, "Marriage Connections among Elite Kin Groups." On Miss Chen, see especially 75–76.
23 (Ming) Lin Jun, "Mulan pi ji xu," *Jiansu ji* (ESKQS ed.), 3:13b.
24 Assuming that Miss Chen's link to Putian and the Mulan dam was through marriage ties, one might well wonder if she had not married into a Putian Lin family; as is explored in *Portrait of a Community*, Chapter 4, several of the Putian Lin patrilines were related to Lin patrilines in Fuzhou.

Finally it was Li Hong, "who was only a rich man," who in 1070 successfully built the dam that survives to this day.[25]

Both the northern and southern farmlands had continued development throughout the imperial era and even up to the present, including refinements to their core waterworks as well as additions along the margins that steadily expanded the area opened to cultivation. As these areas were opened, moreover, they were quickly occupied. For example, drawing on an undated Song source a Ming dynasty account, referring to the retention ponds mentioned above, recalled:

> In 813 the Surveillance Commissioner Pei Ciyuan oversaw construction of an embankment for holding irrigation water that converted wasteland into fields yielding several ten thousand catties [of grain] that supported the prefectural reserves.[26]

Later commentaries noted that the efforts of Pei Ciyuan and others that followed were inadequate in the face of drought, which remained a problem until Li Hong successfully dammed the Mulan and diverted its waters to the areas that lay south of the river. The land to which he provided irrigation quickly attracted new settlers. For example, a biography of Li Hong written in the early twelfth century observed of the Mulan network, "the people overcame the sea and cultivated the land."[27] A similar pattern occurred in the new lands north of the Mulan River, as recalled by Cai Xiang (1012–1067), a notable mid-eleventh century scholar and local native. On visiting his ancestral home Cai inquired about land reclamation projects and noted that "over 8,000 households" already lived on land that had only recently been made available through a network of retention ponds abutting the sea in the "northern farmland."[28]

As beneficial as draining the coastal marshes was to the local agrarian economy, these projects eradicated the habitat that had supported the rich range of marsh creatures. The mollusks, fish and birds that had been so important to the economy of the indigenous peoples, to say nothing of the dangerous animals such as the crocodile, the *jiao* that features so prominently

---

25 A twelfth-century commentator observed that since the Tang the ancestors of Li Hong "had been talented at making money." See Lin Danai (1135 exam graduate), "Biography of Lord Li," *Putian shuili zhi* 7:1a.
26 *BaMin tongzhi* (1989 ed.), 60:411. A late fifteenth-century prefectural gazetteer had the same text, citing an undated Song gazetteer; see *Putian shuili zhi* 5:1b.
27 *Putian shuili zhi* 7:1a.
28 *Putian shuili zhi* 8:11a.

in the story of Wu Xing, were displaced. In their place, the new inhabitants carved out fields, especially the technologically demanding diked paddy that were primarily dedicated to rice. The late nineteenth-century Putian gazetteer says of rice,

> There is "big winter" rice, "early" rice, and "late" rice. "Big winter" rice is planted in the spring and harvested in the winter, and there is only one harvest. "Early" rice is planted in the spring and harvested in the summer. After it is harvested one can stick in "late" rice, thus getting two harvests.[29]

The text goes on to identify a range of more specialized rices that were cultivated on the newly drained land, including glutinous varieties that were especially cultivated for making rice wine.[30] Although the peasants, who had realized the benefits of selecting for specialized traits eons ago, had continued over the many years to refine the grains they planted, already by the Song the variety of rice strains was stunning. But rice was not the only crop. By the late imperial era when the gazetteer was compiled local peasants were also planting millet and wheat as well as beans. The upshot, however, was that the ancient flora of the wetlands was replaced by a narrower range of domesticated crops. Local fauna were also affected as the natural range of creatures was displaced by the domesticated waterfowl, not only ducks but also geese, and domestic animals such as pigs. To collect the marine resources that had once supported the indigenous people, one had to go out into the Xinghua Bay. There, though the waters were shallow, they were open and so more dangerous in the face of coastal storms than the sheltering marshes had been.

Putian were not the only place where coastal marshes were turned into productive farmland. Just to the south, for example, a similar project drained the extensive marshlands that had once defined the mouth of the Jin River in Quanzhou. Further south, in modern Zhangzhou and to the north where the Min River emptied into the open ocean, reclamation drained the marshes that had forced early settlers to abandon initial settlements on the coast and move deeper into the interior, where the rivers flowed freely and fast with

---

29 *(Guangxu) Putian xianzhi* (Taipei: 1968 reprint of 1879 edition), 2:83a.
30 Francesca Bray has written extensively about Chinese riziculture practices. See especially Joseph Needham, *Science and Civilisation in China*, vol. VI, Part 2, "Agriculture," by Francesca Bray (Cambridge: Cambridge University Press, 1984) and *The Rice Economies: Technology and Development in Asian Societies* (Berkeley: University of California Press, 1986).

well-defined channels, to escape the threat of malaria. Nor was transformation of the landscape limited to the coastal salt marshes. The ecology of the upland interior was altered as well as the native forest cover that had sheltered large animals such as tiger and elephant and the myriad smaller animals: snakes, including the feared python as well as poisonous species such as cobra, and birds, was cleared. Wood was needed for construction and for shipbuilding, which was an increasingly important part of the economy as the Fujian coast was progressively tied more deeply to both domestic and oceanic trade networks.

The clearing of the uplands opened new agricultural opportunities. Rice has been the dominant grain across Fujian and all the South since it was first domesticated many millennia ago. However, the ancient strains of rice did best with wet roots and took as long as two hundred days to mature. Some time during the tenth century a strain of rice that ripened in as little as 60 days and was drought resistant was introduced to Fujian from the central coast of modern Vietnam. This so-called Champa rice, named for the local kingdom that was its source, was suitable for the upland fields of the interior where the uneven topography did not lend itself to paddy.[31] Arriving via the increasingly important maritime trade links, Champa rice caught on quickly. Although the grain was considered inferior to the low-land wet root rices that were the staple, it tolerated growing conditions that the more favored varieties could not withstand. That, combined with its rapid growing cycle, made it such an important resource that it came to the attention of the imperial court. An imperial edict issued in 1012 ordered its distribution throughout the inland rice-growing regions of the Yangtze basin.[32]

Champa rice and its subsequent hybridization with older varieties was an important addition to the regional economy, making it possible to spread the cultivation of rice to areas where traditional strains struggled. As a new option, however, it was not alone. A wide range of crops were introduced for the household, including beans and a range of greens, all of which thrived in the new environment of the Plain. Most important to the regional economy, however, was a range of new crops that were aimed at the commercial

---

31 On the arrival and spread of Champa rice, see Ho Ping-ti, "Early Ripening Rice in Chinese History," *Economic History Review*, 2nd series, 9:2 (1956), 200–218. More recently, see Randolplh Barker, "The Origin and Spread of Early-Ripening Champa Rice: It's Impact on Song Dynasty China," *Rice* 4 (2011): 184–86, at https://doi.org/10.1007/s12284-011-9079-6 (accessed 15 September 2021).
32 This narrative can be found in myriad sources, but possibly the earliest is the *Xiangshan yelu*, an undated miscellany compiled no later than the mid-eleventh century by the Buddhist scholar Wenying; see *Xiangshan yelu* b:23b.

market. In the uplands fruit trees such as lychee and longyan, which were dried and shipped long distances both within the empire and beyond, as well as tea, which flourishes in the cooler hills of the deeper interior, all became important. Bananas, which were a source of fruit as well as fiber that was used to make a coarse burlap, and cotton, which became the most important fiber crop after it was first cultivated as early as the tenth century, competed with rice on the Plain as well as in the good bottom lands of the interior.

As the South was tamed, so was it civilized. The civilizing mission was not a one-way process; even today there is an influential residue of the ancient past that redefined what Sinitic means. The non-Sinitic peoples who had lived across the South from time immemorial, however, were either integrated into the Sinitic world, a world that was expanding both physically and culturally, or pushed to the same margins where elephants and tigers survived. The South, in turn, was transformed as it became part of greater China. An essential part of that transformation was economic. Economic development in the South was inextricably linked to the emergence of a network of market towns that evolved hand-in-hand with the evolution of Sinitic culture and the diversification of agriculture. It was through these markets that the exotic products of the South were collected and sent to the great consuming centers that had long existed in the North and that were emerging in the South as well. The growing role of commerce in the economy of the South, however, ran counter to the long-held biases of Sinitic culture, in which commerce and those who profited from it were regarded with a jaundiced eye. Agriculture, as has been explained in Chapter 4, had been the both the cultural and fiscal heart of the economy since ancient times. The mores of Sinitic culture regarded commerce as a derivative and possibly exploitative pursuit through which merchants took the products of peasant labor and turned them into profit. Thus for all the wealth that commerce was pumping into the southern economy, agriculture remained the economic base.

Nevertheless, the upshot was a profound transformation in the ecology of Putian, which stands as a microcosm of what was happening across the broader South. For untold eons, the southeast coast and the uplands that were behind it had been occupied by people who worked in concert with the environment they found. The coast was a world that was rich in marine resources, which the people knew how to harvest. The fringing uplands and the deeper interior provided both additional sources of protein and fruits and other bounty that could be collected. Little evidence survives of agriculture, although that is largely because what evidence might have survived has been wiped out by later development. Regardless, there is little to suggest that those early inhabitants had attempted any systematic or enduring change either to the marshes or to the interior.

The passive acceptance of what nature had given them was inimical to the expectations of the Sinitic settlers whose numbers were growing inexorably through the latter half of the Tang and on through the Song. Some settlers had been pushed by the episodic bouts of turmoil that roiled lands to the north. Others were drawn by the opportunity the South offered. And no doubt some, perhaps even many, of those pushing to transform the land were indigenous people, not immigrants at all but those who adapted to the new Sinitic values. Whatever their reasons, with the growing numbers came a parallel growth in demand for tillable land. In the hill country of the interior this was manifest as the ancient forests were cleared in favor of orchards and terraces. At least as impressive, however, was the impact on the coastal plains where settlement was most dense. Some such land, for example the Jinjiang Plain that lies south of the Jin River in Quanzhou, was already dry and ready to be exploited. But much of the coast resembled the scalloped bay into which the Mulan River and Distributed Blessings Creek disgorged. These were marshlands, the domain of the "floating boat people," the barbarian, and as such they were considered unimproved by the ever more numerous Sinitic agriculturalists. They needed land that could be cleaned of its salinity, where they could have controlled access to fresh water in which to plant their rice. That is what Wu Xing provided, and increasingly the Sinitic model displaced the indigenous.

The result was a reconfiguration of the landscape and ecology as they were remade to suit the needs of the human exploiters. The old topographies of the Putian marsh survive even today in the occasional bumps on the surface of the plain, small hills rarely more than 20 or 30-feet above the broad plain itself, which commonly lies less than 10 feet above sea level. In such places it is not unusual to find villages, often with histories they trace back over 1,000 years. Some barely sat above the tidal line; this would seem to describe the unnamed village at the foot of the mound where the fisherman who found the raft lived. Others sat above the marsh on top of the rises, from where the villagers could tend to orchards and other crops aimed at the market. Baidu Village, for example, that sits just north of the Putian district city atop a hillock on the edge of the Plain, has been renowned for its orchards of lychee and longyan since it was first settled in the late Tang. Many, including Baitang Village that was the home of Liao Pengfei whose text is central to the preceding chapter, sat on the newly drained land itself.

It has been many centuries since the marsh has been transformed into the Plain of Emerging Transformation. Today traces of the marsh itself have largely been lost with all the ecological change that has resulted. The crocodiles are gone, pushed to the still wild coastlines of the Southeast Asian archipelago lands. Maladies such as malaria, schistosomiasis and yellow fever, although still present, are at least understood, and with understanding can be addressed. The Plain today is densely settled with an economy that mixes agriculture with modern industry. The ecology on which the ancient indigenous people depended is no longer to be found.

Chapter 7
CONCLUSIONS

As has been explained in the opening chapter, our story illustrates a process of cross-cultural engagement and economic transformation from a very local perspective that by the end of the first millennium CE had been widely underway across the broader South for many decades, even centuries. There was no standard process, no local model that can stand alone to illustrate how this engagement played out from place to place. The common feature across the South, however, was the interaction between the array of culturally and ethnically non-Sinitic cultures that had long occupied the land from time immemorial and the intruding Sinitic model that had evolved from the ancient culture of the Central Plain, an engagement that led to a profound change in both.

When this process began, as early as the Han dynasty if not even in the latter stages of the Zhou era, the diverse cultures and politics of the Yangtze River basin and the coastline south of the Shandong Peninsula were very different from those of the Central Plain. Over the course of the first millennium CE this changed as the disparate cultures of North and South engaged and cross-influenced each other. Our story comes rather late in the broader process. For a variety of reasons: mountain barriers, indifferent soils and indigenous hostility toward immigrants, among many, the more narrowly defined littoral regions south of the Hangzhou Bay and east of the Pearl River estuary, including both the coast and the interior highlands, attracted only a small number of the early Sinitic migrants. They primarily followed the interior river basins, which bypassed the area known to early scholars as Min. It was not until the mid-centuries of the first millennium CE that the Sinitic presence began to have a noticeable impact, and it was not truly until the turmoil and migration associated with the mid-eighth-century rebellion of An Lushan that has been referenced several times in earlier chapters when that presence became defining.

A reader might well ask, in light of this, what makes this particular story, a very local story that does not even include all of Min, worthy of focus? For one thing, I have long found it an interesting story that speaks in many ways to the lives of people in a remote past. It is exactly the kind of story that historians search for, a story that allows us to peer past history's common focus on the lives and doings of a narrow elite. Equally significantly—perhaps even more so—it is a story we can access. Because it occurred rather late in the broader transformation of the South, it is better documented than similar stories elsewhere.

Across the South the levels of political and technological sophistication varied widely both in space and time. Along the middle and lower reaches of the Yangtze River and the fringes of the Hangzhou Bay rice had been cultivated for several millennia and was already a major crop by the Han dynasty. Some of the earliest pottery in human history has been found in the middle reaches of the Yangtze basin, and many of the southern cultures had mastered metallurgy. Indeed, some of the finest swords of the pre-imperial era were cast by southerners. The urban center at the mouth of the Pearl River estuary that was once known as Panyu and for the past 1,500 years as Guangzhou was already an important port by the time of the First Emperor in the late first millennium BCE. Some argue that it was his desire for the exotic goods for which the South was already famous that spurred his campaigns of conquest through the Yangtze basin and beyond. Elsewhere powerful kingdoms: Wu, located in the littoral region of modern Jiangsu province north of the Yangtze River; Chu, which dominated the central basin of the river; and later Southern Yue, which controlled the deepest South for a century, had begun to engage the courts of the Central Plain demanding coequal status. The Wu kingdom of the first millennium BCE had even presumed to be the hegemon leader of a coalition of Central Plain courts. The South was not a primitive wasteland.

The central Fujian coastline where Wu Xing battled the *jiao*, however, was among the least sophisticated regions. Below the Min River basin of northern Fujian state structures were weak to nonexistent and technology, including both in casting pottery and metallurgy, remained primitive. Moreover, while across the South drainage of riverine, lakeside and coastal marshes was common, Wu Xing's battle with the *jiao* has no parallel. But the broader themes illustrated by the Distributed Blessings drainage project: the transformation of untamed lands into agriculturally productive fields and paddy, the accompanying displacement of traditional economies with an agricultural economy and the valuation of Sinitic culture over an indigenous culture that allowed the latter to survive unchanged only in the territorial and cultural margins, were not unusual. They are, in fact, an essential part of the processes that transformed the South from an alien land to one that was increasingly a part of the Sinitic sphere.

A key point to recall, however, one that I made in the opening chapter, is that none of this had to happen until it did. At any moment in the historical narrative, only the past is teleological. What has happened cannot un-happen, a fact no historian can ignore. At the same time, that which had not yet happened did not have to, a reality no historian should overlook. Consider again Wu Xing's encounter with the crocodile that undermined the embankments on which his project relied. The indigenous people of the coast had lived with crocodiles. Nature provided, but nature was not always benign. Crocodiles were part of the bargain the people had with the natural world in which they lived, just as were the sharks of deeper water, as well as the pythons and tigers of the interior. They were the non-benign aspects of nature with which the indigenous people had always shared their space. But the narrative does not recall the crocodile as a crocodile. It was a *jiao*, a legendary and predatory beast. And it challenged Wu Xing's project to transform the environment.

Wu Xing's project, of course, went forward. The environment was transformed. The question is: Why call the beast a *jiao*? Why not simply call it a crocodile? Why claim, as the later narratives do, that Wu had implausibly battled the beast for three days before both were dead? Why not recall the event as it really occurred rather than transform the crocodile into something numinous and so inherently even more dangerous than the reality? There is, of course, no irrefutable answer to any of that. It is certainly plausible that Wu Xing swore he would kill the beast that was undermining his dikes, that he had died as he fought and killed the crocodile, and that it took three days to find Wu's body. Yet none of that would explain why the beast is remembered as a *jiao*. Han Yu did not, in the name of the emperor, order *jiao* to leave Chaozhou; he ordered crocodiles, for which he had a perfectly good word that to this day means "crocodile," to leave.

These are questions to which we can never know the answers for certain, but perhaps the *jiao* should be seen as an allegorical manifestation of indigenous resistance. Note that the indigenous people are absent from the narrative we receive. The anonymous people who Wu Xing addressed as he prepared to engage the beast have no identity. Wu spoke; they heard. But we do not know who "they" were. Were "they" the Sinitic immigrants and the acculturated indigenes for whom Wu had drained the marshlands? Were "they" cheering Wu on? Or were "they" non-acculturated indigenes who were losing their livelihood as the marsh was drained? Perhaps "they" did not passively accept the transformation of the world that had supported them for time untold. Perhaps instead "they" had resisted Wu's attempts to drain the marsh. And perhaps "they" had cheered the crocodile that indeed was undermining Wu's network of canals.

Of course, none of that is a fact; all is the ahistorical "perhaps." Yet there is a reality behind those questions. Wu Xing did not eradicate the indigenes who had lived beside and on the marsh. Recall Yue Shi's comment in his *Universal*

Geography of the Taiping Era, first mentioned in Chapter 4: "The *quan lang* are the barbarian households of the prefecture." Yue Shi identifies the *quan lang* specifically as the survivors of Lu Xun's abortive attempt to carry on Sun En's rebellion. Although Yue says they had "scattered across the mountains and seas," he adds that they are known as the "floating boat people," and further noted, "They commonly live aboard their vessels and move about with the seasons. They have no fixed abode." These, in short, were the descendants of the non-Sinitic indigenous people who had been displaced by the Distributed Blessings drainage project. While some no doubt had found refuge in the interior highlands as Yue Shi recalled and from where they had done battle with the encroaching Sinitic settlers,[1] those with whom he was familiar had found refuge on their boats as they floated among the off-shore islands. Two centuries after Wu Xing had completed his project, they were still there.

The orthodox narrative proposes that the world of the *quan lang* was entirely subsumed by the Sinitic world that Wu Xing embodied. But that was not the case, as is clear from the story of the Divine Woman of Meizhou Mazu, the "Maternal Ancestor," recounted in Chapter 5. Her roots were with the non-Sinitic indigenous people of the central Fujian coast—the *quan lang*. She was not a Sinitic deity. But her cult was not constrained by her origins. In fact, she became one of the most important deities in the Chinese world. Her cult spread wherever the *quan lang* traveled: Up and down the Chinese coast, then across the waters to Taiwan and Southeast Asia, and ultimately to far-flung destinations such as Los Angeles, San Francisco, New York and London—all places where the descendants of the *quan lang* have traveled and settled. Of course, she is not identified as the deity of a long-forgotten non-Sinitic culture; she is a Chinese deity. And that in turn leads back to the historiographical issues which we introduced in the opening chapter.

The modern Chinese state, the People's Republic, dominates the contemporary map of East Asia. It is the premise and consequently the policy of that state that every region embraced within the outlines of that map is Chinese territory eternally, no matter how recently it may have been absorbed by the empire. Such culturally and linguistically disparate areas as Tibet and the oasis communities of Xinjiang in the far west are part of the Chinese empire today. So is Taiwan, a part of the Chinese cultural world yet so profoundly different from the mainland. The state asserts that they will remain part of the empire forever. As unyielding as the contemporary state is about these areas, however, even Chinese scholarship recognizes their distinct history;

---

1 See Hugh R. Clark, *Sinitic Encounter with Southeast China through the 1st Millennium CE* (Honolulu: University of Hawaii Press, 2015), 117–122.

there is little risk in acknowledging that, so long as that acknowledgment does not challenge the legitimacy of the Sinitic empire.

This is less true about the area that is the central concern of this book: the greater South. The South is irrefutably an integral part of China today. It is difficult to imagine it will not remain so far into the future. The more tangible challenge is to recognize that it has not always been so. There is little risk in the modern state in recognizing that once upon a time the South was culturally, linguistically and politically distinct. However, since the orthodox narrative emerged in the later centuries of the first millennium CE, in the face of extensive evidence to the contrary it has maintained that the distinct South of long ago was culturally deficient, politically undeveloped and economically backward. When the South was absorbed by the First Emperor late in the first millennium BCE it was the fulfillment of a long latent imperial mandate. Perhaps the First Emperor had used force to bring the South under the empire's control, the narrative acknowledges, but the benefits that accrued were so obvious that there was little resistance. In fact, it cannot be denied that southern resistance to an accommodation with the Sinitic world eventually ceased. Thus Sun En, whose rebellion at the turn of the fifth century that has been raised in Chapter 4, was not the hero of southern identity in the face of northern hegemony but a barbarian who sought to obstruct the flow of history. The peoples of the South, the narrative presumes, wanted to be part of the emerging empire. Consequently, it treats the centuries of division that followed the collapse of the Han dynasty early in the third century CE as an aberration. The South was integrally part of the realm; any attempt to reverse that—even if temporarily successful—was a denial of that.

This illustrates both presentism and teleology, the two historiographical themes that were discussed in Chapter 1. Late in the sixth century, as was outlined earlier, the centuries that followed the collapse of the Han empire that have been labeled the "Era of the Northern and Southern Dynasties" came to a close with the southern campaigns of the emergent Sui/Tang empire. Although a latent southern culture persisted and even persists today to an attenuated degree, the empire was once again politically whole, as the narrative presumes it should be. The distinct and separate South of the pre-imperial era, it asserts, could not endure. The force of history must teleologically lead to the integration of North and South. Furthermore, whether an observer's present was the mature Tang of the eighth century or the People's Republic of the twenty-first century, the present seems immutable. The unified, or "holistic," empire is and always will be. But …

What if history had not unfolded as it did? What if a distinct southern identity had proven stronger than the northern desire to subdue it? What if an integrated empire unifying the Central Plain, the Yangtze River basin and the associated coastal littoral had never proven stable? None of those outcomes occurred, and the historian cannot write an alternative history. But could that have happened? Consider the centuries that followed the Han, that "Era of the Northern and Southern Dynasties" that endured for three-and-a-half centuries—much longer, one might note, than any of the modern countries of the Americas have endured so far, including the United States. The southern empire was viable.

During these centuries a succession of courts claimed control of the South from the Huai River basin that marked the border region separating North and South to the Red River delta in what today is northern Vietnam.[2] Initially, the ruling elite of these courts relied overwhelmingly on expatriate northerners such as Wang Hong. Even men who, though born and raised in the South, could nevertheless argue that their ancestor had migrated from the North several generations earlier were largely excluded from access to authority. Recall the story of Tao Kan, a native of the South who was dismissed by a northern grandee as a country bumpkin although he claimed a northern heritage. Men such as Tao Kan were marginalized by the northerners who monopolized the halls of political power. Even more, there was no room in those halls for those who were truly indigenous, men like Luo Qisheng who had no claim to northern heritage and who found themselves at best limited to marginal roles on the frontiers of orthodox civilization. It was the alienation between native southerners and the immigrant elite that led to a number of uprisings in the name of southern identity.[3]

In time, however, in the southern empires the barriers between North and South weakened. If the fourth-century Eastern Jin court against which Sun En rebelled relied almost entirely on expatriate northerners, the sixth-century Chen dynasty, the last of southern dynasties and the one that was conquered by the armies of Yang Jian and the Sui dynasty in 589, had deeply integrated southerners, both descendants of early Sinitic immigrants and those with an indigenous background.

Southern elites were familiar with many of the cultural premises of the Sinitic North. They read the same body of classical texts; they too embraced the ideology that today we call Confucian. Elites in North and South had embraced Buddhism as well as the nativist challenge of Daoism. Yet the South in the decades before the Sui conquest had its own distinct identity.

---

2 See Lewis, *China Between Empires*, and Chittick, *The Jiankang Empire in Chinese and World History*.
3 Although the rebellion of Sun En is arguably the best known example of southern resistance to northern hegemony, it is not alone. See Clark, *Sinitic Encounter*.

CONCLUSIONS

Southern scholars read the classical texts, but they developed their own interpretations. Southerners of all types embraced Buddhism, but their Buddhism was heavily influenced by masters who came from the oceanic South rather than the overland routes of the North. And across the South devotion to the panoply of local and regional gods and the associated indigenous rites and festivals such as those that celebrated the "Maternal Ancestor" remained central to peoples' lives.

The Sui/Tang empire technically endured for over three centuries into the opening decade of the tenth century. Its authority, however, had already been deeply compromised by the mid-eighth-century rebellion led by An Lushan before it was thoroughly shredded in the last decades of the ninth century by the rebellion associated with Huang Chao discussed in Chapter 5. One of the oft-neglected features of the Sui/Tang empire, however, is the enduring cultural and political split between North and South. Political power belonged to the former; economic power, however, was increasingly dominated by the latter. Few southerners succeeded in the imperial examinations; most who aspired to an administrative career instead were tracked into the southern selection examinations that have also been introduced in Chapter 5.[4] No later than the early ninth century, however, and arguably well before then, the Yangtze basin had become the economic heart of the empire.[5] As a final attempt to assert a distinct southern identity, when the last Tang emperor finally abdicated in 907, across the South independent courts were established.

Of course southern expressions of distinct identity did not lead to a politically separate South. The independent courts of the tenth century one by one were absorbed either by force or submission to the Song dynasty that arose in the later tenth century. When the Song court lost the Central Plain to the invading Jurchen people who established their own Jin dynasty in the twelfth century, it was forced to find sanctuary in the South. In marked contrast, however, to the centuries between the Qin/Han empire and the Sui/Tang empire, when the courts of the Yangtze basin were largely content with their lot, the refugee Song court never abandoned its vision of a restored holistic empire. It was, ironically, the Mongols who finally accomplished the restoration, but except for transitional moments of political upheaval the empire has never been split since.

---

4 For a fuller discussion of this, see Hugh R. Clark, *China During the Tang-Song Interregnum, 878–978: New Perspectives on the Southern Kingdoms* (London: Routledge, July 2021).

5 See Clark, *China through the Tang-Song Interregnum*, chapter 4, "The Economies of the South."

The South today is deeply integrated into the Sinitic empire, but not because it was overwhelmed by a greater culture. And that leads us, ultimately, back to Wu Xing and his battle with the *jiao*. The project launched by Wu Xing to drain the marshes, like innumerable similar projects across the South, did transform the environment. Neither the *jiao* nor the *quan lang* could forestall that. What did happen, on the other hand, was an accommodation between North and South, and accommodation that changed them both. This is illustrated by the cult of Mazu, the Maternal Ancestor. The cult persists to the present as a reminder that Chinese culture is not simply the ancient Sinitic culture but one that has accommodated numerous local and regional cultures. In the Maternal Ancestor, both the *jiao* and the *quan lang* still survive.

SUGGESTIONS FOR FURTHER READING

Contemporary Chinese scholarship has generated a rich body of local history. Among the many works on the early history of Fujian one might note Zhu Weigan, *Fujian shigao* (Draft History of Fujian), two volumes (Fuzhou: Fujian jiaoyu, 1985 and 1986) and the several works of Xu Xiaowang: *Fujian tongshi* (Comprehensive History of Fujian), four volumes (Fuzhou: Fujian renmin, 2006), *Fujian minjian xinyang yuanliu* (The Development of Popular Beliefs in Fujian) (Fuzhou: Fujian jiaoyu, 1993) and *Mazu de zimin: MinTai haiyang wenhua yanjiu* (The Offspring of Mazu: Research into the Maritime Culture of Fujian and Taiwan) (Shanghai: Xuelin, 1999).

The cultural encounter between the Sinitic world of the Central Plain and the diverse cultures of the South has only recently begun to generate attention in both Chinese and western scholarship. Among the more significant of the former is Jiang Bingzhao, *Dongnan minzu yanjiu* (Research on the People of the Southeast) (Xiamen: Xiamen daxue, 2002). Two ongoing publications: *Zhongguo Yuexue* (Chinese Studies on the Yue), edited by Wang Jianhua and *Dongnan wenhua* (The Cultures of the Southeast) offer additional insights.

Among the works in English Edward H. Schafer, *The Vermilion Bird* (Berkeley: University of California Press, 1967), a brilliant review of Tang literati perspectives on the South, deserves special mention, both for its exceptional scholarship as well as its easy accessibility. Several general works were written before much of the Chinese scholarship, including Harold Wiens, *China's March to the Tropics* (Hamden, CT: Shoe String Press, 1954, updated and reissued in 1967), Wolfram Eberhard, *The Local Cultures of South and East China* (Leiden: Brill, 1968, a translation of *Lokalculturen im alten China* [Brill, 1942]) and Charles Patrick Fitzgerald, *The Southern Expansion of the Chinese People* (New York: Praeger, 1972). Although dated and supplemented by more recent scholarship, all three offer useful insights. These have been ably supplemented and updated in Mark Elvin, *The Retreat of the Elephants: An Environmental History of China* (New Haven: Yale, 2004) and Robert B. Marks, *China: An Environmental History*, 2nd edition (London & New York:

Rowman & Littlefield, 2017), synthetic approaches Chinese history through the prism of the environment; although the coverage in both is comprehensive, there is much excellent material on the South. D. Jonathan Felt has considered the north/south dichotomy from the perspective of geographic discourse in *Structures of the Earth: Metageographies of Early Medieval China* (Cambridge, MA: Harvard University Asia Center, 2021).

An essential discussion of the political and cultural history of the era of division is Mark Edward Lewis, *China Between Empires: The Northern and Southern Dynasties* (Cambridge: The Belknap Press of Harvard University Press, 2009). Lewis's work has been ably and equally essentially complemented by Andrew Chittick, *The Jiankang Empire in Chinese and World History* (Oxford: Oxford University Press, 2021) and the *Cambridge History of China*, volume 2, *The Six Dynasties, 220–589*, edited by Albert E. Dien and Keith N. Knapp (Cambridge: UK: Cambridge University Press, 2019).

Recent western scholarship with a narrower focus on the Southeast and Fujian include Jiao Tianlong, *The Neolithic of Southeast China: Cultural Transformation and Regional Interaction on the Coast* (Youngstown, NY: Cambria Press, 2007), a deeply researched review of the Neolithic cultures of the Fujian coast, and Erica Brindley, *Ancient China and the Yue: Perceptions and Identities on the Southern Frontier* (Cambridge, UK: Cambridge University Press, 2015), the first synthetic treatment in English of the pre-Sinitic peoples of the Southeast. See also the collected essays in *Imperial China and Its Southern Neighbors*, edited by Victor Mair and Liam Kelley (Singapore: Institute for Southeast Asian Studies, 2015).

Several recent books have focused on local religion in Fujian. Notable are Brigitte Baptandier, *The Lady of Linshui: A Chinese Female Cult* (Stanford: Stanford University Press, 2008), which focuses on a cult that arose in the interior of northern Fujian in the late Tang, and Kenneth Dean, *Taoist Ritual and Popular Cults of Southeast China* (Princeton: Princeton University Press, 1993). Although both are primarily concerned with later times than are the focus of this book, they have good information on the origins of cults. Both therefore complement Valerie Hansen, *Changing Gods in Medieval China* (Princeton: Princeton University Press, 1990), which traces the transformation of several cults, including that to the Mazu, the Maternal Ancestor, as they spread widely through the empire.

Finally, there is the array of my own work on which the arguments in this book rest. Much has been cited in the course of my discussion, but I would mention specifically *Portrait of a Community: Society, Culture, and the Structures of Kinship in the Mulan River Valley (Fujian) from the late Tang through the Song* (Hong Kong: The Chinese University Press, 2007), *The Sinitic Encounter in Southeast China through the First Millennium CE* (Honolulu: University of Hawaii Press, 2016), and "What's the matter with 'China': A Critique of Teleological History" (*Journal of Asian Studies* 77:2 [2018], 295–314).

INDEX

An Lushan (and Rebellion of) 15, 19, 55, 81, 87
Austronesian (& Proto-) 11

Baidu & Baitang Villages 78
bamboo rafts 35, 70
Ban Gu 9, 51
banana 66, 77
Bao He 65–66
Buddhism 86–87

Celestial Masters 12
Central Plain x, 1, 4, 6, 8, 10, 14, 31–32, 43–44, 49, 53, 55, 59, 63, 65, 81, 82, 85, 87, 89
Chaozhou 24, 26–29, 66–68, 83
Chen Li 68
Chinese characters 49n9
cholera 68
Chu *guo* 8–11, 82
Confucius x, 1, 7, 8
crocodile 27–30, 40–41, 67–68, 75, 78, 83; *see also jiao*
cultural exchange, x

Daoism 7, 8, 27, 38–40, 86; and rebellion 12, 40
Distributed Blessings Retention Dam & Stream 17–23, 32, 50–52, 60, 67, 70–72, 78, 82, 84; Creek 17, 21, 72, 78
Divine Woman of Meizhou 60–63, 69, 70, 84, 88
dragon/*dracos* 24–26

ecology: *see* landscape
elephant 37, 65–66, 68, 76–77
Empress of Heaven: *see* Divine Woman of Meizhou

Fang family (of Putian) 59–60
First Emperor 12, 82, 85
"floating boat people" 35–36, 50–51, 69, 78, 84; *see also quan lang*

Fujian ix, x, 5, 15, 17, 24, 26, 29, 37–40, 59, 60, 72, 73, 76, 82, 84; indigenous cultures of 32–35, 51; infectious diseases of 68; population of 52–53, 56–57; wild animals in 66–68
Fuzhou (Fujian) 32, 39, 57, 73; *see also* Min River
Fuzhou (Jiangxi) 47

gazetteers 20n4
Goujian 9–11, 49
Grand Canal 14
Gu Yong 44–45
Guangzhou 10, 29, 43–44, 46, 50, 68, 82

Han dynasty 4, 9, 12–13, 40, 43–46, 48–51, 81, 82, 85–86; *see also* Qin/Han empire
Han Yu 24–29, 40, 67, 83; "Offering to the Crocodile" 28, 67
Hangzhou & Hangzhou Bay 10, 33–34, 44, 48, 49, 66, 81, 82
Hu Fan 46–47
Huang family (of Putian) 58–59

immigration & settlement 15, 43–44, 46–47, 78
In Search of the Supernatural (Soushen ji) 37–39
indigenous culture & people 3–4, 10, 12–14, 17, 38–39, 42–47, 49–52, 57–59, 61–63, 68–70, 74–75, 77–79, 81–84, 86–87; displacement of 5, 43, 48, 84; registration of 15, 52–53, 56; *see also* "floating boat people"; *quan lang*

Jiankang: *see* Nanjing
Jiao/jiaochi & *chi* ix–x, 22–30, 40–41, 67, 75, 82–83, 88
Jin dynasty (12th century) 87
Jin dynasty ("Western" & "Eastern," 3rd–5th centuries) 24, 44, 46–48, 57, 86
Jin River: *see* Quanzhou

INDEX

Jiulong River & basin 32–33, 52, 56

Koguryo 61
Kong Fuzi: *see* Confucius

Lady of Dawu (*Dawu furen*) 39–40
landscape 65–66, 83; coastal marsh ix, 17, 19, 21, 33, 34, 36, 55, 68–72, 74, 78; topography & ecology ix, 71, 76–79
Legalism 7
Li Bing 22n9
Li Chunfeng 29
Li Fu 62
Li Shizhen 25
Li Zhen 62
Liang dynasty 55
Liao Pengfei 60–62, 69, 78
Ling Shun-sheng 35
Lingchuan district (Putian) 36–37
Liu Kezhuang 20n4, 20–23
Liu Song dynasty 44, 47
Liu Zongyuan 24, 28, 65–67
longyan: *see* lychee
Lord Master of the (Daoist) Law (*Fazhu gong*): *see* Master Zhang
Lu Xun 50–51, 84
Lu Yundi 61
Luo Qisheng 46–48, 86
lychee 66, 77, 78

McNeill, William 15
malaria 68, 76, 79
man (ethnicity) 10, 46, 47, 67
Manchus 4–5
Master Zhang 38–39
Mazu: *see* Divine Woman of Meizhou
Mengzi 7, 51
Min River & basin 32, 33n3, 34, 37–38, 56–58, 73, 75, 82; *see also* Fuzhou (Fujian)
Mongols x, 3–5, 87
Mozi 7
Mulan River & basin 21, 32, 41, 51, 52, 56, 60, 69–70, 72–74, 78

Nanjing 13, 14, 44, 45
Neolithic x, 10, 27, 33–36, 40, 69
non-Sinitic culture: *see* indigenous culture & people
North China Plain: *see* Central Plain

Ouyang Xiu 17–18, 68
Ouyang Zhan 26, 26n25

Panyu: *see* Guangzhou
Pearl River 10, 81, 82
Peng Cheng 66
Peoples Republic of China ix, 2–4, 84, 85
Plain of Emerging Transformation 17, 52
population 5, 15, 39, 50, 52–53, 55–57, 72; and immigration 39, 41; indigenous 12, 47–48, 53; *see also* Fujian, population of
presentism 2–4, 30, 85
Putian district 17, 19, 32, 52, 56–62, 68, 71, 73, 75, 77, 78
python: *see* snake

Qin dynasty 7, 11–12, 14, 40; *see also* Qin/Han empire
Qing dynasty 5
Qin/Han empire 13, 14, 87
Qu Yuan 22n11
quan lang 50–51, 61, 63, 69–70, 84, 88; *see also* "floating boat people"
Quan/Zhang satrapy 56
Quanzhou 24n18, 26–27, 29, 32, 35, 38, 39, 50, 55, 60, 61, 66, 69, 75, 78; population of 52

Record of the Grand Historian (*Shi ji*) 24, 40–41
Red River 8, 86
rhinoceros 65–67
riziculture ix, 11, 33–34, 51, 75–78, 82; Champa rice 76

St. Elmo's Fire 61
schistosomiasis 68, 79
Shandong 8, 9, 12, 81
Shang dynasty 1, 6, 8, 10
(Shu) Han *guo* (3rd century CE) 13, 24
Sima Qian 9, 10
Slash-and-burn agriculture: *see* Swidden agriculture
snake 25, 29, 37–39, 41, 65, 66, 76
Song dynasty 44, 50, 55–56, 60, 63, 66, 71, 75, 78, 87
southern selection examination 58–59, 87
Southern Yue (*guo*) 82
Sui dynasty 5, 13, 14, 85–87; *see also* Sui/Tang empire
Sui/Tang empire 13, 87
Sun En 48–50, 85, 86
Swidden agriculture 15, 34

INDEX

Taiwan 5, 11, 35, 38, 84
Tang dynasty 4, 14, 15, 17, 20–21, 24, 47, 53, 55–57, 59–60, 68, 71–72, 78, 85, 87; *see also* Sui/Tang empire
Tang-Song Interregnum 55–56, 60, 72
Tao Kan 45–46, 86
Tao Yuanming 45
Teleological history 2–3, 30, 83
Tibet 3–4, 84
tiger 24, 37, 65, 66, 68, 76, 77, 83

Universal Geography of the Taiping Era (Taiping huanyu ji) 35, 50, 83–84

Wang Hong 44–45
Wang Mang 43
wasp 49, 49n9, 66, 68
Wei *guo* 13
Wei River & basin 6, 11
Wu Guang 23, 10
Wu *guo* (10th century) 82
Wu *guo* (Three Kingdoms) 13, 44–48
Wu *guo* (Zhou dynasty) 9, 10
Wu Xing ix–x, 17–23, 26–27, 29–30, 41–42, 41n22, 50–53, 55, 57, 60, 68, 70, 72–73, 78, 82–84, 88
WuYue *guo* (10th century) 66

Xinghua Plain: *see* Plain of Emerging Transformation
Xinjiang 4, 84
Xunzi 7

Yang Jian 13, 86
Yangtze River & basin ix, 1, 3, 8–10, 12–14, 33–34, 40, 43–48, 50, 55, 57, 76, 81, 82, 85, 87
yellow fever 79
Yellow River & basin x, 1, 6, 31, 43; *see also* Central Plain
Yellow Sea 61
Yellow Turbans 12
yue (ethnicity) 10–11, 47–48
Yue *guo* 9–10, 40, 49; *see also* Goujian

Zengzi 7
Zhang Hua 46
Zhangzhou 24, 27, 32, 39, 52, 66, 75
Zhejiang 10, 59
Zheng family (of Putian) 57–58
Zhongguo 6–9, 11–14, 31
Zhou (Latter 10th century) 56
Zhou Chu 22, 22n9
Zhou dynasty 6–11, 81
Zhuangzi 8
Zuo Si 24

www.ingramcontent.com/pod-product-compliance
Lightning Source LLC
Chambersburg PA
CBHW030142170426
43199CB00008B/178